My Purpose

vs

God's Purpose

For My Life

By
Martin G. Howard

My Purpose vs. God's Purpose: For My Life

Printed and bound in the United States of America
ISBN 978-0-615-66396-8

TABLE OF CONTENTS:

Dedication

First I would like to dedicate this book to Jesus Christ, my personal Lord and Savior. For without Him dying for my sins and giving me the gift of eternal life, none of this would be possible. I also dedicate this book to my beautiful wife, Zoé. She has been by my side through thick and thin. She was there with Jesus giving me the strength I needed when I was weak.

Our beautiful daughter, Isabela, who in her own right is a miracle. Isabela was born 3 months early, weighing only 2 pounds 5 ounces. Against the odds, she proved all of the doctors wrong. They told us that if she was born before 30 weeks she probably would not make it; she was born at 27 weeks. She had a brain hemorrhage when she was in the Neonatal Intensive Care Unit (NICU). The doctors told us that she would be a slow learner and behind all of her classmates. Again, she proved them wrong.

And our handsome son, Samuel, who was named after the prophet of the Old Testament. During my wife's pregnancy with him, she was reading the book of 1Samuel. We were trying to decide on a name.

She told me she felt that God wanted us to name him Samuel. We agreed to pray on it.

About a week or two later, I was at work and talking to someone about our son; I referred to him as Samuel. Almost immediately, I sent a text to my wife letting her know that I felt Samuel should be his name. Little did I know she too was talking to someone, at that very moment, about the name Samuel. We knew then that would indeed be his name.

God has saved us and delivered us from our circumstances. We owe Him everything, for without Him we are nothing.

Introduction

This book is about yearning questions we have throughout life. It has been designed as a helpful resource for those who are searching or those who might be sliding in their faith. We all have a purpose in life. Some days I know what mine is; while others I am unable to make heads or tails of it. The truth is that nothing has changed in God's eyes. God has a plan for each of us. Of course, we also make plans of our own. The problem is that the plan that we have is not always the same as the plan that God has for us. It is during those days, when my plan and God's plan for me do not match up, that I cannot figure out what my purpose is. I felt I was going down the right path, and then something happened to make me think I was not only on the wrong path, but that I was not even in the right park.

Prayer is the way to ask God what He wants for you. Remember, you must not only pray and believe, but it is just as important to act on your prayers. If you are in a dead-end job, with no opportunity for advancement, praying for more pay or more responsibility might not happen in your current situation. If you want more pay or more responsibilities, you might try applying for a different position. That reminds me of the story of the two farmers. The ground was drying up due to a long drought. Every morning the farmers would pray for rain. Even though they both prayed for rain only one of them actually went out and planted crop seeds. Are you going to pray for a miracle and do nothing? Or, are you going to pray for God's blessings and prepare your fields for the rain? James refers to this idea quite often in chapter two of the book that bears his name. "Faith without works is dead…" (James 2:26; NKJV)

Chapter 1: "If I don't know what my purpose in life is, how could I possibly know what God's purpose is for me?"

"Many are the plans in a person's heart, but it is the Lord's purpose that prevails." (Proverbs 19:21; NIV)

Perhaps you are someone that wakes up every morning and you ask yourself, "Is this what I want to do for the rest of my life?' If you do not know what you are supposed to do with your life, how could you possibly know what God wants you to do with it? It could be that you are waiting for something miraculous to happen. Something that will explain everything you are destined for. Would you listen if it was laid out like that? Take Jonah for example. He was content with his life just the way it was. However, God had other plans for him. When He spoke to Jonah and told him to go to Nineveh, Jonah high-tailed it and ran away as fast as he could.

In the world we live in now, I do not know of anyone who would do less than freak out if they were in Jonah's shoes. Imagine you are in the middle of a good sleep and in a dream God tells you that He has a plan for you. He tells you to go to the large city, Nineveh in Jonah's case, and tell everyone there that they were sinning against God. To put it a little more into perspective, God comes to you in a dream and tells you to travel to New York City and tell everyone that they need to change their ways.

Most people, in general, rank speaking in public scarier than dying. Not only are you to speak in public, but you are to tell this very large city, and their king, that they are doing wrong in God's eyes. Yeah, that would probably scare most of us. Not to mention the possible beatings you might receive in return. Personally, I know I would probably run as fast and as far as I could; just as Jonah did.

Of course, since God is the one in control, He was able to convince Jonah. Being swallowed whole, spending three days in the belly of a whale, and then being spat up on the shore would be enough to convince most people. It was enough to convince Jonah as well; he did exactly what God had asked him to do. God's purpose for your life might never come to you in a dream. It is possible that you may never fully understand what your purpose in life is. But, God knows what His purpose is for you. As a believer, you will be used for His purpose whether you know it or not.

Your purpose in life is already planned out for you by God. He knows when you will be born, what your name will be, and the people He will put around you. He knows everything that you will do in life; the great accomplishments you will make. Be aware though, He has given each of us the blessing/curse of freewill. In a moment of self-centeredness you might reject His blessings for you. When you realize that you are not in control, but rather God is, life will be much clearer. Just remember, you are called to be one in a million and not one of a million.

Chapter 2: "My Wife Has Her Purpose"

"Take delight in the Lord, and He will give you your heart's desires." (Psalms 37:4; NLT)

If you are reading this, then at some point in your life you have more than likely questioned why you are here. You might have even questioned why you believe what you believe. Maybe you even questioned your very existence in this life. I have asked myself all of these questions many times. Believe me, there are many days when I do not feel I contribute anything to this world. Perhaps I am here just to muddle through life and then die. Then again, maybe I am here to be a beacon of light to someone else.

For years, I had been going through life not knowing if I even had a purpose. I believe that we are all here for a purpose, a reason, and I continue trying to figure out what mine is. I am sure you have met many people in your life where it was apparent that they have a purpose; my wife is a prime example of such a person. She is a social butterfly. Saying that she loves to talk might be an understatement. But, anyone who has ever met her would also know that she is genuine.

A number of years back, my wife went through a major transition in her faith in the Lord. She was raised Catholic, but she was never taught the concept of having a personal relation with God. That is not to say that others who are raised Catholic are taught in the same manner. After learning that having a relationship could change her life, she was all for it. In April 2007, she accepted Jesus Christ as her personal Lord and Savior and followed in believer's baptism.

Since that day, she has become a steward for the Lord. She happily shares her story with others and many have since become believers. One of the gifts that God has given my wife is the gift of evangelism. Through that gift, she has been able to realize and accept God's purpose for her life.

In the beginning, Adam and Eve had the greatest purpose in all of mankind. "...and God said unto them, be fruitful, and multiply, and replenish the earth, and subdue it: and have dominion over the fish of the sea, and over the fowl of the air, and over every living thing that moveth upon the earth." (Genesis 1:28; KJV)

God laid out His purpose for Adam and Eve. Throughout the Bible there are countless examples of God telling people what His purpose was for them. But, what about the rest of us who do not receive that divine intervention? Those of us who do not have a burning bush that speaks to us? Or, an angel that appears in a dream to give us guidance?

There is also the possibility that we are blessed for not receiving that divine intervention. God calls on all of His children to believe in faith and spread His Word to the masses, but He calls on specific individuals for something divine. The list of these who have received and answered the call is great, but when God calls He asks for everything. He does not ask for your brief moments in the morning before you eat your breakfast. Or that two minutes when you thank Him before falling off to sleep. No, God wants it all. In return for your submission, His reward will be more than you could ever imagine.

Unfortunately, not many in today's society, including yours truly and other devoted Christians, are willing to give up everything in order to answer God's calling. My friend, God is not asking you to give up everything for Him. God is not asking you to give up anything that He has deemed good for you. He does not want you to be penniless, no home, no family, no food, and no clothes. That is not what God asks for. He wants you to want Him more than your home, more than your family, more than your clothes, and more than your money.

In order to find your purpose, you will need to ask Him through prayer. Your purpose might be something that is apparent to you immediately, or the answer might be staring you in the face and it will still take you many years to figure out. You must open your heart and mind to be receptive to the message that God is trying to send you. This is why it is important to interact with other Christians, go to church, read your Bible, and pray. When your heart and your mind are open to understanding, then you will see what He is trying to tell you.

One problem that I believe our country suffers from is lack of guidance spiritually, morally, and ethically. Not necessarily from the church, but from prominent figures in society. For instance, during the Clinton administration, Bill Clinton taught us that it is okay to commit adultery and lie about it. In the end the American people, Congress, the courts, and the rest of the world felt that it was okay for the President of the United States, the most powerful man in the world, to lie to the world with no repercussions.

In today's society if you have moral, ethical, a strong belief system, and integrity you are punished for standing up for what you believe. But, that must not stop you, or me, from standing firm in the Christian principles and beliefs. Just because they jump off the cliff, does not mean that we should too.

The rest of this book, I have looked at some

questions and statements that I have received from believers and non-believers throughout the years. Along with some topics that will help us all to look at life through a different lens. It is my hope that you will be able to relate to one or two of them. Through your reading, my wish is for your heart and your eyes to be opened to what God has already put before you.

Chapter 3: "Why should I believe in the Bible?"

"For I am not ashamed of the gospel of Christ, because it is God's power for salvation to everyone who believes..." (Romans 1:16; Holman CSB)

For a non-believer, this is a completely legitimate question. As for those of us who are believers, we know that there is a clear answer. Before I get to the biblical answer to this question, I want to look at a non-biblical answer. For years, archaeologists and scientists have either tried to prove or disprove the Bible. Just think for a moment about what they are trying to do. If the New Testament was written two thousand years ago, then it would suffice to say that the Old Testament is much older than that.

Unless I am mistaken, there is no one currently living who is two thousand years old. Therefore, we have to rely on the words of those who have come before us. I love watching a popular channel dealing with the history of the world. During one show, they had a special device that was able to see the bottom of the Red Sea; the body of water Moses and the Israelites crossed after leaving Egypt as they were being chased by the Pharaoh and his army. At the bottom, they found what appeared to be the outline of chariots. It was very interesting to see how marine life had grown on the chariots yet their silhouettes remained the same.

On another show, they had found what appeared to be the twin cities of Sodom and Gomorrah. As I watched these shows I was fascinated in two different ways. As a man who enjoys learning about history, I was fascinated with watching these crews uncover historical events from thousands of years ago. And, as a believer, I enjoyed watching these people prove further what the Bible had already stated.

That takes me back to my point about no one being at least two thousand years old; the Bible already spoke of the sin cities of Sodom and Gomorrah which were struck down by fire. Additionally, the Bible had already spoken of the Pharaoh and his army being drowned by the wall of water, in the Red Sea, after Moses led the Israelites through it to safety. The scientists were not proving anything, but rather reaffirming what the Bible had already stated.

From a biblical perspective, the Old Testament prophets made over four hundred prophesies of the coming and life of Jesus Christ. And He fulfilled each and every one of those prophesies. From where He was born, how He would live, how He would be betrayed and killed, how He would plead for the forgiveness of those who persecuted Him, and how He would be raised from the dead. The odds of anyone else being able to fulfill every one of those prophesies would be impossible. There are several reasons why it is the number one selling book of all times.

Chapter 4: "Why should I believe in Christianity?"

"And Jesus answered him, It is written, Worship the Lord your God, and serve Him only.'" (Luke 4:8; Holman CSB)

Some things never change. The world in which we live today is much like it was throughout the Old Testament. Back then, the world was full of different religions and gods. The paganism which I am referring to is the act of polytheism; or the belief of numerous gods. Greek mythology is a classic example of this with each of their gods having special powers.

Unfortunately, this practice plagued the prophets of the Old Testament as well as Jesus in the New Testament. When Moses went up on Mount Sinai, the Israelites began worshiping a former pagan god. Without their leader, the Israelites became lost and needed direction, just as people today are seeking direction in the multitude of religions. In the United States, and perhaps the world, money has become the most worshipped god. Money has taken over as the most powerful force of the world and its people. Individuals, companies, and countries, strive to gain the most money as a symbol of their status and success. When money becomes the object of your affection, you have in essence chosen money to be your god.

Christianity is based on the teachings of Jesus Christ; which is focused on God's law. God's law starts with the Ten Commandments given to Moses on Mount Sinai. Jesus then added to what the great leaders had taught in the Old Testament. It is important to understand the Old Testament since during Jesus' time on earth that was all they knew.

Jesus spent a majority of His life learning and discussing the Old Testament with elders. He spent His last three years spreading the Word through healings, miracles, compassion, and love to the rest of the world; those are the years that are most documented and therefore most known. His apostles would carry on His story long after He was crucified on the cross, was raised from the dead three days later, and soon thereafter ascended into Heaven.

As Christians, we continue to believe what God has taught us, through His word, that there is only one true God. Jesus walked the earth two thousand years ago. His stories have been passed down from generation to generation. No matter what the skeptics say, we believe that He was the Messiah who was sent from God to earth in order to teach us how to live and to love. Jesus was not only here to teach us, but He was also sent to die for us; for our sins.

As a Christian, I believe that God the Father sent His son, Jesus Christ, to earth to die for our sins. Through faith, I believe that He is my savior and my trust is in Him. We have the right to choose from many gods; however, as with any decision we make in life, there are consequences for our decisions. In this case the decision to worship false idols. As Christians, we believe that there is only one true God.

Chapter 5: "I want to believe in Christianity, but I'm just not ready." (For those who are seeking)

"Then Jesus said to those Jews who believed Him, If you abide in My Word, you are My disciples indeed. And you shall know the truth, and the truth shall make you free." (John 8:31-32; NKJV)

Becoming a Christian is not like ordering food from a restaurant. Yes, there are many religions out there to choose from. However, becoming a Christian is a life-altering decision. In chapter five of 2 Corinthians, Paul tells us that once you decide to believe and follow Christ you become a new creation. As a new creation, who and what you were no longer matter. You have been given a new start in a new life.

When we decide to accept God and His son Jesus Christ into our life, we have decided to change our lives forever. Because of this, we cannot accept them and continue to live in sin as we had prior to that acceptance. Our lives not only will change but they must change. That is not to say that we will never sin again because we will. It means that we will no longer have to face sin and temptation alone.

It is a common misunderstanding that all one needs to do is be a good person to be saved. Even an atheist can be a good person. So we must be careful not to fall into the belief that being nice is all we need. We do not want fall into the trap of the blind leading the blind. That is to rely on another new believer to help strengthen our faith. I would recommend that we surround ourselves with Christians who are strong in their faith.

It is important to be aware of self-proclaimed Christians who yell, scream, and even hold up signs in order to make others believe. We are told, in numerous locations throughout the Bible, not to argue/quarrel with others. We are to spread God's Word to those who are willing to listen. Not to force His Word onto others. Besides that, we cannot make someone else believe; it is a decision that will be made when the Holy Spirit enters into their life.

As Christians, all we can and should do is to plant seeds into people's hearts. Once the seed is planted, the Holy Spirit will grow the seeds within them. As the seed grows, the eyes of the non-believer will be opened to see the glories of His Kingdom. We cannot force this to happen.

The decision to become a Christian is one that must be made individually. However, I can share with you why I chose to accept Jesus into my life. I was raised in a Christian household. I knew that every Sunday morning, I would be going to Sunday school and then listen to a Sunday sermon. Sunday night, it was back to church again for youth group. Wednesday nights we were back again because my parents sang in the church choir. At a young age, I started singing in the children's choir and later transitioned into the youth choir. Going to church was a part of my life.

Every summer growing up, my parents sent me to a youth church camp. At age thirteen, while at camp, I accepted Jesus into my life and followed in believer's baptism. I thought I knew everything I needed to know in order to be a Christian. However, as I got older I began to question what and why I believed. Think about it, if there are so many religions out there, how is it that Christianity is the one true religion to follow?

In high school, I became curious about other religious beliefs. I asked myself, why do others practice their religion and not Christianity? Just as Jesus was on earth, some of the other religions were based on actual human beings that walked the earth. However, there is one major difference between Christianity and any other religion; Jesus Christ still lives. There is no other religion that can say that. But more importantly, Christianity is not about a religion but rather a relationship.

Becoming a Christian is not always the popular thing to do. In many countries, people are killed just for professing that they are Christians; even in the twenty-first century. As Christians, we have rules and attitudes that we are instructed to live by. And when we die, we are judged by how we lived our lives. For instance, after you learned the truth, how many people did you share it with? Or, did you keep it all to yourself? It is like having the cure for HIV or cancer. How would you feel if you knew that someone had a cure for a deadly disease/virus and did not share that knowledge with anyone else? Pretty upset I am sure.

Sharing the gospel with others is the same thing. Jesus promised eternal life to those who believe. If you believe that Jesus Christ is the son of God, confess that He came to the earth to die for your sins and mine. If you believe and trust in Him and His word, then you too will live in God's glorious Kingdom for all eternity.

Once you become a believer, Satan will do everything he can to win you back. We live in a world that will tempt you beyond your personal strength. Everything that is in the news, on the internet, on the television, and in your daily lives will tempt you to stray from your beliefs. Our society has accepted the idea of separating religion and state. In the United States, we have accepted foul language, lewd actions, even partial nudity (full nudity in other countries) on broadcast television. Christian or not, we cannot get away from the fact that our world is getting closer to being where it was prior to the great flood. This country is becoming like the biblical cities of Sodom and Gomorrah. Remember what happened to them?

But, with the great flood and the burning of the cities, God saved those who loved Him. We have allowed too many non-believers to tell us how we should live our lives. It is time that we live for God and not for them. God speaks the truth and we need to listen. We have the opportunity to live in eternity with our savior; all that is required of us is to say yes to His calling. Will you say yes today?

Chapter 6: "Why go to church when they're all just a bunch of hypocrites?"

"If a brother or sister is without clothes and lacks daily food, and one of you says to them, Go in peace, keep warm, and eat well,' but you do not give them what the body needs, what good is it? In the same way, faith if it does not have works, is dead by itself." (James 2:15-17; Holman CSB)

The best response to that question is something that my pastor said during a sermon one Sunday morning. He said that people do not go to a hospital when they are well. No, they go when they are sick. In the same way, Christians are sinners and therefore go to a place to help them to be well again. A church is full sinners. Many times over, they walk out the front door only to sin again; perhaps before they even reach their cars. It is an unfortunate truth, but a truth nonetheless.

It all began with the fall of Adam and Eve. Once they sinned against God, by eating the apple from the forbidden tree, we are all now born into sin. Then Jesus came to earth to live a sinless life and die a sinner's death in our place.

The church is also full of individuals who are Christians by affiliation not by faith or practice; they claim to be a Christian but fail to act like one. Perhaps they do not tithe, read their Bible, or they simply do not act in a manner which would be termed 'Christ-like'. Someone who has a filthy mouth, is sexually immoral, an overall mean person, and the like. I am not passing judgment because at different points in my life I too fell into this category.

In the same way we are hypocrites in and outside of the church. If a person goes to church, but only associates with certain individuals, perhaps they should ask themselves the question, 'do others know I am a Christian by what I claim to be or by how I act?' The people we surround ourselves with probably make us feel comfortable, but sometimes those friends are not a good influence. During the time of Jesus, He was traveling with His disciples through Samaria. Jesus went over to a watering well to speak to a woman there; His goal was to save and not condemn.

The Samaritan woman had a very colorful background; married five times and was currently living with a man who was not her husband (John 4). During that time, those two things were a big no-no. First off, to the Jews, Samaritans were like an inferior race. And for a woman to have a colored past, she would have been considered an outcast to society. However, Jesus came to save the lost and the weary.

Jesus did not come just to talk to the Pharisees, the rich, or those in government. He came for the lost; whether they were rich or poor. Jesus came to help a leper be with his family again; to help a blind man see; to help a lame man walk; and to help a dead man live again.

As Christians, we try to live our lives in a way that is 'Christ-like'. So, will you be a Christian by faith or by affiliation? If a man/woman/child is without food, will you not lend a helping hand?

It does not matter our background, our religious beliefs, or the country in which we live; as humans we are selfish. As Christians, we are taught time and time again to love thy neighbor as thyself. Our neighbor can be anyone, not just that person who lives near us.

Christians may be perceived to be hypocrites because of the way some act. Some may go to church every Sunday. They may know every hymn and every verse in the Bible. But, outside of the church they may be very mean to all those around them. Maybe they curse a lot and speak in derogatory terms to others. Whatever it is, they are not acting in a manner which is 'Christ-like'.

We will never walk a life that is equivalent to Jesus Christ. God knows that we will sin and fall short of His glory. That is why He sent His son to walk on the earth, to show us how to live and worship, and eventually die a sinner's death in our place. In return, He asks that we believe and trust in Him. Believe that He sent His son Jesus Christ to die on the cross for our sins. Trust that He has a plan for us. Then go, spread the word of the Lord to others so they also may believe.

The best way we can spread the Word is through our actions. Being a nice person to those around us is a good start, but we cannot stop there. Our actions speak much louder than our words ever could. If we are gossipers or people who like little cliques, we should try to treat everyone as equals without isolating or playing favorites. A great example of this would be the men Jesus chose to be His twelve disciples. Jesus knew that Judas would betray Him and that Peter would deny Him. However, He loved them just as He loved the others. And, He loved them just as much before they betrayed Him as He did after they betrayed Him.

Will we choose to be a steward of the Word or just an affiliate? God sent His one and only son to the earth to die on the cross for your sins and mine (John 3:16). What have we done for Him lately?

Chapter 7: "The Bible was written two thousand years ago. How can it possibly relate to life today?"

"In the beginning was the Word, and the Word was with God, and the Word was God." (John 1:1; NASB)

This is the type of question from someone who doubts why they should believe in the Bible. But, one must understand the context in the stories of the Bible rather than the time in which it was written. What I mean is that throughout the history of the world our advancements as a race has changed; thus the way we live our lives too has changed. Yet, many things are still the same as they have always been.

For instance, in the story of David and Goliath, King Saul offered David his personal sword, armor, and shield to protect him. Being a wealthy man, King Saul was able to afford the best sword, shield, and armor a blacksmith could make. I am sure the crafts-manship was excellent. His sword was probably etched with a beautiful design created specifically for the king. His shield was probably sturdy and strong, able to deflect the striking of an opposing sword. And, his armor was most likely thick enough to stop a flying arrow or the slashing of an enemy sword. In any case, it was the best 'advanced technology' money could buy.

Let us go back even further in biblical history. When Moses led the Israelites out of Egypt, we know that the Pharaoh and his army were chasing them on chariots. A chariot was a horse drawn carriage that was designed for military leaders. That being said, not everyone had chariots to ride on. They were reserved for high ranking officials rather than the common man. Of course, the technology of the chariot advanced to carry numerous people and/or supplies and equipment. In time, man would create vehicles to replace the horse drawn carriage.

Through any of the above scenarios, one could see that in today's society we see the same types of situations. The best advanced technology costs a lot of money; many times only the wealthy are able to afford. And often, our military are the first to have the latest high tech fighting equipment, which later enters into the public sector. The stories are very similar if you take the advancements of men into consideration.

Back to the story of David and Goliath. David was a small young shepherd boy. He was nothing like his brothers or the rest of the men who were military warriors. But, he was the only one willing to face the exceptionally strong and tall man on the enemy's side. Goliath would have been an advanced military warrior with numerous victories under his belt. To this day, we still use this analogy when comparing two opponents.

If you understand the context of these examples, then it is clear that it does relate to our lives today. They had kings and we have queens, presidents, prime-ministers, and dictators. The similarities, we still have a supreme ruler over us. We still live in a world where people will believe in whatever they want to believe. Our world is full of people who are unwilling to listen to the truth. We know that God flooded the earth and destroyed cities with fire because of such people. In recent years, we have had cities and countries decimated by hurricanes, earthquakes, and tsunamis; one of the cities was known for its sinfulness.

Even though the Bible was written two thousand plus years ago, it does not mean that we are to take His Word lightly. If we understand the reason in which it was written, then it is clear that it does pertain to us more than we are willing to accept. If the Word was before time began, then it will be there long after we are gone.

Chapter 8: "I don't go to church because all they want is my money!"

"If God will be with me and will keep me on this journey that I take, and will give me food to eat and garments to wear, and I return to my father's house in safety, then the Lord will be my God. This stone, which I have set up as a pillar, will be God's house, and of all that You give me I will surely give a tenth to You". (Genesis 28:20-22; NASB)

It is unfortunate that people believe in this statement. However, it is more unfortunate that the impression is even out there. Most likely, someone actually went to a church where this mentality was upheld. Yes, churches need money in order to operate. The church is a place to worship, but it is also a non-profit business. As technology advances, so do many of the churches. With technology, many churches are going to on-line giving or installing collection stations in the common areas; this is done to eliminate the passing of the offering plate.

Too often people forget that the church is also a business. As a business, the church has employees and bills that need to be paid. Of course, that does not include the different missionaries or organizations the church might support. We all go to work, either for someone else or for ourselves. We work because we have bills to pay, food to buy, and miscellaneous stuff we want to spend our money on. The church is the same way. The bills are to keep us warm during the cold of winter; to keep the lights on during a midnight service on Christmas Eve.

We buy food to nourish our bodies; the church provides food to nourish our souls. We buy gifts for others that they might enjoy them; the church spreads the message of the greatest gift of all. Yes, the church asks you for money. But, they only ask for a small portion of what God has already provided to you.

I used to be under the false understanding that I made my own money. 'I go to work every day, I work long hours, and I should be able to keep what I make.' That is the wrong attitude to have. God put everything in motion for our lives; from beginning to end. We got the job because we were the best applicants, and we were the best applicants because God put us in the right jobs to receive the proper training. He was preparing us for where we are right now and where we will go in the future.

Back to the tithing and why God chose a tenth of our income to be considered our tithe. There are many numbers that are very special in the Bible. Forty was a very popular number in both the Old and New Testament. Moses and the Israelites fled from Egypt for forty years. Noah built an ark to escape the flood for forty days and forty nights. And, Jesus fasted for forty days and forty nights; during which time He was tempted by Satan.

The number twelve is another important number in the Bible. There were the twelve Disciples of Christ and twelve tribes of Israel (the twelve sons of Jacob). My wife's favorite number in the Bible is three; the Father, the Son, and the Holy Ghost. And of course the mighty number seven. There were also numerous other instances of these numbers being represented throughout the Old and New Testament.

With all of these other numbers of great significance, why would He choose ten to represent our tithing? Well, it began with Abram (before he became Abraham). He was blessed by the high priest Melchizedek, King of Salem (Genesis 14:17-20). In return, Abram gave him one-tenth of everything he achieved from the defeat of his enemies.

It came up again during the time of Jacob, in his journey from Beersheba to Haran. During his journey he stopped to rest for the night. During his sleep God spoke to him making a promise to bless him and his descendants. When he awoke, Jacob took the rock from under his head and made it into an altar to God. He vowed to give God a tenth of all He would give him (Genesis 28).

The New Testament does not talk a lot about the tenth being the requirement. However, it is understood that in the New Testament there are certain things that are implied. More importantly, it does refer to the idea of being a cheerful giver. Therefore, when we give back to God, He asks that we give unto Him as a thanksgiving and not out of requirement. Additionally, most churches only ask for tithing from their members and not guests.

Chapter 9: Quote from a husband. "I don't mind if she is the head of the household."

"Wives, be subject to your own husbands, as to the Lord. For the husband is the head of the wife, as Christ is also the head of the church..." (Ephesians 5:22-23; NASB)

As much as many guys would love to hand control over to their wives, we must not yield to that temptation; even though at times it might seem to be the easier way. In the beginning, God the Father, God the Son, and God the Holy Spirit were creating the universe. It was decided to make man in the image of God (Genesis 1:26).

Being made in His image means so much more than just what you see in the mirror every morning. God is the supreme ruler over the universe, so shall you (husband; father) be ruler over your household. In Genesis, God told man that he will not only have control over his household, but every living creature on the earth. He gave us reign to watch over the world; to maintain and protect it. This is how we should take care of our household too.

I have talked to a number of couples who experience this very situation. The wife wants the husband to be the head of the household and take control, but the husband is afraid to do so. Not necessarily because he is weak, for it is in our very gene to be the protector. He might feel this way because he is afraid of being criticized for making a mistake. However, being the head has two major parts to it. Not only to make the decision and tell the body what to do. But, the head must also listen to the body in order to make such decisions.

I have explained it like this. The husband is like the President who appears to be the one making the decisions. The fact is he is being advised what to say and how to say it from others in the background. In this example, those people in the background would be the wife. Wives are to support, encourage, and be a friend to your husband. Behind every powerful man is a supportive and intelligent woman. Part of that role is to help him make and understand decisions for the family. The power of a man comes from the strength of his family which includes himself.

Husbands and wives should learn their roles in the household. Just because the husband might not want the role of 'head of household' does not mean that the wife should take it from him. It is irrelevant if the wife believes she could do a better job. Plain and simple, it is his job.

I love to watch football. There are times when I find myself watching a game in which my team is losing. It is in those moments that I feel that I would be a much better quarterback than the one on the field. But, that is not my job. Plus, I am sure if I suited up, I would get the snot knocked out of me. Oh, I know I could lead some pretty good game winning plays. And if I did, it would not be because of me; it would be because of the team I had behind me. But, I also know that there is a reason why I am not in that position.

Wives, I have a suggestion for those who think they have all of the answers. Share those ideas with your husband. I am not saying to tell your husband what to do, but rather suggest what could be a good idea. If he is to step up and take the lead, it is important for the wife to move into the second spot.

Back to the football analogy, I am not the coach but I might suggest a few plays. Perhaps the coach might even listen to one or two of my suggestions. In the end though, it is his team and not mine. He makes the final decision; right or wrong. If the team wins, it was a group effort. But if the team loses, then it has to be the coach's fault. Wives should understand and acknowledge that the family, and the household, is under the husband's direction. Wives are encouraged to give suggestions, advice, and guidance. Just remember, in the end it is his team (1 Timothy 2:11-13).

If you are a single female and find yourself in a relationship, this information also pertains to you. Since you are in a relationship, you should still work toward taking on your individual roles. The lady in the relationship should begin to assume the role she would play within the marriage. The man should also begin to assume the role that he would play within the marriage. For most people this is pretty natural. However, this might be a little more difficult for those who are extremely independent or co-dependent. Either the guy does not want to step up or the lady does not want to step down. But, if you both want your relationship /marriage to work, each of you should accept your positions within the partnership.

For single mothers out there, not in a relationship, right now you are the head of the household. You do not have a man to assume that role. When you do get into a serious relationship, you should allow him to assume that role. If you maintain the attitude of, 'he can be the head of his household and I will be the head of mine' you are setting yourself, and the relationship, up for failure.

Chapter 10: "Where was God when __________?"

"No one will be able to stand up against you all the days of your life. As I was with Moses, so I will be with you. I will never leave you nor forsake you." (Joshua 1:5; NIV)

I do not know what your (fill in the blank) statement would be. I know what mine would be and there would be many. Where was God when I lost my job because I reported numerous company safety violations? Or, where was God when I left the military and found myself unemployed with a family to care for?

No matter what you think, whether it was something that happened to you or someone you know, God is not the one to blame. Perhaps it is your fault. I know we do not like to point the finger at ourselves. It is much easier to blame someone else. Since God is the creator of all things, why not blame Him? Wrong. God loves each and every one of us, simply because we are His. He made us in His image. However, He also gave us the gift of free will. That means we are given the opportunity to choose to love Him and obey His commands. Or, we can choose to do things the way we want to do them.

Here is a scenario for you. A man is driving down a two-way street. He gazes over to look at a very attractive young lady walking on the sidewalk. Unfortunately, he failed to see the car that pulled out in front of him. There was an accident, but thankfully no one was hurt. Now, was God involved in any of that?

The man is driving and not paying attention to the road but rather to a nice looking lady. Was God telling the man he should not lust after another woman with his eyes? What if the guy was single, he has every right to find his mate. Was it God telling him to keep an eye on the road? God does not control our daily lives in that way. God had nothing to do with this accident. He did not have the car pull out in front of him to teach him a lesson. If that were the case, how many women would get into an accident while applying their makeup on the way to work? Or those who like to text and drive (or talk and drive)? If a person cannot talk and remain in their lane while obeying the speed limit, then they should put the phone down and concentrate on the road.

There is no doubt that God is with us everywhere we go. He even tells us in His Word. Sure, we might not be going out to conquer a city, or lead a nation out of oppression. But, we will face trials throughout our lives; maybe we will face a trial at least once a day.

We will never be able to compare our pains to the pain that Job went through in his life. It definitely was not Job's fault what had happened to him. But in His wisdom, God allowed it to happen. God does allow us to go through trials in our lives. But, He will never give us anything more than what we can handle. It might seem like we are moving a mountain, but in God's eyes we are merely opening a door.

Jesus told us that on earth we will have trials and sorrows (John 16:33). We should believe that He will help us through them. In Romans 5, Paul tells us that the trials we go through are for our benefit.

Again, God is with us always. However, He should not be the blame for everything or anything that goes wrong in our lives; not everything will be of God's doing. We could be facing a hardship because of something we did and this is the effect of our decisions. It could be the workings of someone else; someone who just does not like us and wants bad things for us. Unfortunately, even Christians are guilty of this one; envy is a sin. God allows things to happen, even if they seem to be bad in our eyes. He puts us through trials so that we may grow. If we ask God for patience, He will give us plenty of chances to learn patience. Then again, it could merely be just one of those things that we will never understand and therefore will go unexplained. And I do not believe that God had anything to do with it. Some things just fall into the category of bad things happen to good people.

Chapter 11: **"That was God telling you not to do that!"**

"'You speak as a foolish woman speaks,' he told her. 'Should we accept only good from God and not adversity?' Throughout all this Job did not sin in what he said." (Job 2:10; Holman CSB)

How many times has something not gone your way, and somebody chimes in, 'well, that was God telling you not do to that!' I believe that is merely a scapegoat of an excuse that people use to justify things that do not go right in their lives.

A young lady was at a party with some friends drinking. After a while, she began to throw up. Is that God telling her she should not drink? No. God teaches us not to be drunkards; this includes drugs. We should only be addicted to three things: the Trinity (the Father, Son and Holy Spirit), your spouse and children, and your family and friends. These should be our only loves. In this example, it was simply the young lady's body was telling her she had too much to drink.

God was not telling the young lady not to drink.

The body was only designed to drink so much. In the time of Jesus, wine was a common drink; actually it was the safest thing to drink. Jesus even turned water into fine wine.

God does not want us to fail, but rather He wants us to live in abundance. That is why He gave us His laws and sent His son to die for our sins. Look what Jesus Christ was able to do through the apostle Paul; once a self-proclaimed blasphemer, persecutor of the early Christians, and a violent man (1 Timothy 13-14). However, God also gave us free will to make our own decisions. God is not trying to control our lives, unless He specifically tells us to do something. He shows us the right path to take. Throughout our lives, He puts us through different circumstances that we may learn from those experiences. Through those experiences we gain knowledge. It is through that knowledge that we are able to make the choices for our lives, but it is ultimately our decision to make the best choice.

Chapter 12: "It is because of my hard work that I have such wonderful things. It was all me!"

"*You may say to yourself, 'My power and my own ability have gained this wealth for me,' but remember that the LORD your God gives you the power to gain wealth, in order to confirm His covenant He swore to your fathers, as it is today.*" *(Deuteronomy 8:17-18; Holman CSB)*

How many times have you felt that everything you have was because of the fruits of your labor? I know that I am guilty of that. I used to believe that the harder I worked the more I would receive. Unfortunately I was very wrong. How is it possible that one man can work twenty-three hours a day and still not have all that he needs? On the other hand, there is another man who skates through life without lifting a finger, yet has more than anyone could ever need or want. Did God bless the second man more than the first?

In the book of Daniel, we read of a very powerful man who had everything a man could want. He had worked hard to receive it and was able to enjoy the fruits of his labors. However, God had to open

Nebuchadnezzar's heart and mind to realize what Daniel had told him. In Nebuchadnezzar's second dream, he was a tall and strong tree with many branches and beautiful leaves. But, in his dream the tree was broken down and his leaves were scattered throughout the land. In Daniel 4, Daniel explained that King Nebuchadnezzar would lose his reign and be forced to live the life of a peasant if he continued a life of sin.

In 2006, I experienced something similar when the railroad moved us out to Utah. First of all, we did not want to move there. But, that was where we had to go if I wanted the promotion. He had a plan to move us closer to Him. I ended up working for a very mean man who made every day at work a living hell. The worst part, he claimed to be a fellow Christian. On top of that, we were in an area without many Christian churches; only Mormon churches. I understand that many Mormon's believe that they are Christians. I do want to be somewhat sensitive here. If we understand the Bible, then we know that the Jesus in the book of

Mormon is not the same Jesus.

The basis for Christianity is the life, death, and resurrection of the Lord Jesus Christ. While in Salt Lake City, we had the opportunity to go to the temple grounds. I noticed that there were plenty of pictures and statues of Jesus, but there were no crosses. I asked one of the tour guides what the reason was for this. She explained that the cross is representative of a bad thing that happened to Jesus and they only wanted to remember the good things. So, they only wanted to focus on the life of Jesus, but not His death and resurrection. We know that His death and resurrection is the foundation of Christianity.

Even though we did not like the location, I had worked hard to receive that promotion. The promotion came with a $10,000 pay raise and opportunity for bonuses and greater promotions. I was proud of myself and what I had accomplished; that pride would prove to be my failure. Throughout it all, I do not think I ever praised God for His guidance. I felt it was all me.

When I lost that job, I lost more than the sole income for my family; I lost the identity I had created for myself.

But, just like Nebuchadnezzar, things began to turn around for me when I acknowledged that God was the one in control. I have not made it back to where I was professionally, but I have far surpassed where I was as a Christian.

That brings me to the second man. Why are some more prosperous than others? God provides prosperity to those who call upon Him. However, God never said that money is the only form of prosperity. God does not give money as a reward for good servitude. If that were the case, thousands of people, if not millions, would all simultaneously win the lottery. Prosperity could be in the form of friendship and love. One can have all the money in the world, but without friendship or love they would be very lonely. And despite what the movies say, money cannot buy us love. Look what happens to wealthy people with their big groups of 'friends' that hang around them. As soon as they lose the money they also lose their so-called friends.

Our society relies heavily on money as a form of status in society. Unfortunately, not everyone can be blessed with monetary wealth. The world is comprised of those who have monetary wealth and those who do not. God teaches that He will prosper those who will trust in Him. It is important to remember that the Bible does not teach that money is the root of all evil but rather the love of money (1 Timothy 6:10).

While Jesus was here He taught us if a man loves his money, he will not get into the Kingdom of Heaven (Mark 10:25). Understand, He never said that He will drop a suitcase full of cash at your doorstep. Nor does He say that we will have a relative leave his /her wealth to us. Prosperity through God does not mean money or property. If you are looking to be prosperous in money and property then those things of the world have become your god. God promised to provide for His people; and He does. For those who He does bless with property and monetary wealth, He puts conditions into it. If the wealth becomes more important than Him then He will remove the temptation.

Nebuchadnezzar was restored to power when he acknowledged that God is the Most High and has dominion over all (Daniel 4:36).

Chapter 13: "My friend goes to church. He says that he's a believer, but he doesn't act like one."

"For we must all appear before the judgment seat of Christ, that each one may receive the things done in the body, according to what he has done, whether good or bad." (2 Corinthians 5:10; NKJV)

Unfortunately, we all live with the curse that Adam and Eve put on us by eating the fruit of the forbidden tree. We are all disobedient in some way or another. To add insult to injury, we make excuses or blame others for our actions. Adam blamed Eve, and Eve blamed the serpent. To this day, we blame others for our actions. 'It is all my parents fault. Because of them, I never got involved in my school.' Or perhaps, 'it is society's fault that our children are so disobedient. Parents can't even discipline their children without getting into trouble.' And, of course, 'the devil made me do it'.

Why do we continue to go down the path of blaming others for our faults? We study history so we can, in some way, predict what the future will hold. So, why can we not learn that blaming others only makes the problem worse? Okay, so we blame a co-worker for not finishing the project on time. What are the odds that the co-worker of which I speak will want to work with us again? We have now complicated our situation further. We all mess up now and then. It is a lot easier to admit when we are wrong and move forward; as opposed to making excuses or lying to make ourselves look better. We messed up and now feel that we have to lie to cover up our shortcomings. Perhaps we should have made a better decision in the first place.

In Paul's second letter to the church in Corinth, he states that we will be judged by the things we do; 'good or bad.' How many of us can honestly say that we look at both the positive and negative outcomes of a situation? I am a realist, so that is the way I function naturally. My wife does not seem to understand my logic much of the time, but she accepts the way that I am. We all need to look at both the positive and negative outcomes of a situation. If the negative outweighs the positive, then most would agree not to go that route. Unfortunately, it is measuring the weight of the negative over the positive where we get into trouble.

If a person is married, and has had an affair, they should ask themselves if they had analyzed the possible outcomes. God told us that committing adultery is a sin. Of course, that would be one obvious outcome. But much deeper, they had actually committed two sins. Long before they actually had physical intimacy, they had been mentally or emotionally intimate; they had lusted for the other person.

At that point, they had broken two of the Ten Commandments. And they probably made up an excuse for their actions. 'My wife just doesn't understand me.' Or, 'my husband is never there when I need him.'

When we get married, we took a vow to each other. Remember, that vow is also to God. We are to: be loyal to that person, to cherish in both sickness and in health, and the commitment would be until death. 'But, society says that one out of every two marriages will fail.' Are we marrying society? Or, are we marrying that person who sees us as the one they could not live without?

God knows our strengths and our weaknesses. He knows the great things we will do with our lives, and the sins we will commit. King David sings of this in Psalms 69.

If we just stand by and watch our friends make this transformation, then we are not being a true friend or follower of Christ. As Christians, we are also a support system for one another. We all face the devil and his evil deeds throughout our lives. Because we are believers, the devil's desire to have power over us is greater than for a nonbeliever. Therefore, we should strive to help each other to remain vigilant against the devil.

Unfortunately, there are two types of Christians. On one hand, there are Christians who go to church every week like clockwork. Every Sunday morning, they wake up and go to church. Perhaps they praise and they worship the Lord. Once the service is over they leave the church and go back home. They go and put a check mark on their 'I go to church' list. And for the rest of the week, they do not live or act as a believer of His word. Without passing judgment, we need to remember that a church is like a hospital, it was built to care for the sick.

On the other hand, there are Christians whose every day is filled with helping others. Perhaps they help others through acts of kindness, or merely passing along kind words. They show their love for the Lord in everything they do. They are like the pillars of the church; cemented and sturdy in God's word.

Moses went up to Mount Sinai to receive God's law that he might tell others. As Christians, we have received the Word of the Lord through the church, our pastors, fellow Christians, and the Holy Bible. We are commanded to spread the Word to others so they may be saved as well. Do not forget to share and remind fellow Christians as well. For we share the Word of the Lord because of love. Not only because we love the

Lord, but because He loved us first (John 3:16).

We are to love our friends and help them to do what is right. But, the ultimate decision is in their hands. We can lead a person to the truth, but they have to accept it for themselves.

Chapter 14: "I know it's wrong, but I can't help myself."

"The godly are directed by honesty; the wicked fall beneath their load of sin." (Proverbs 11:5; NLT)

This is something that everyone faces; both believers and nonbelievers. Actually, there is far more temptation for the believer. Nonbelievers do not always understand what they are doing is wrong. Whether we are believers or not, we have convinced ourselves that what we are doing is not wrong. We make excuses for it to make it okay in our mind. Perhaps we have talked a little too long to someone of the opposite sex at work; even though one of us is married. We make excuses for it by saying it was 'work related'; even if the conversation merely took place at work.

Believers face the same challenges; the difference is that Satan wants us to fail. Satan will go one step further by giving us an excuse for it. Because we want to believe it we will, as if the excuse will make the wrong go away. When we are married, lusting for that co-worker is adultery in God's eyes. If we identify ourselves as believers, then we should already know this. Finding a person of the opposite sex attractive is not a sin; there are many very attractive people out there. It is when we cross the line from finding them attractive to lusting after them. When we begin creating scenarios in our mind that go against our marriage vows, it is then that we have crossed the line (Matthew 5:28-29).

As believers, we know that God is omnipresent; meaning He is everywhere at all times. In our hearts, our mind, in every breath we take, and every thought we make. The term, 'the devil made me do it' is a lie that we sell to ourselves. If the Bible says that God is omnipresent, then how is the devil able to get into our mind? That is the true test of our faith. I believe that the devil does plague our mind. The devil does entice us to have sinful thoughts. Perhaps one could say that he puts them into our head (Romans 1:21).

As believers, we fight this very battle every

waking moment. We are constantly faced with temptations. And we make excuses when we heed to those temptations. Instead of relying on our own power, we should let God help us fight that battle. The temptations will be great, but the power of the Lord is much greater than anything the devil could throw our way (Joshua 1:9).

Chapter 15: "I have changed for him, but he won't change for me!"

"Why do you look at the speck in your brother's eye, but you don't notice the log in your own eye? Or how can you say to your brother, 'Brother, let me take out that speck that is in your eye,' when you yourself don't see the log in your eye? Hypocrite! First take the log out of your eye, and then you will see clearly to take out the speck in your brother's eye." (Luke 6:41-42; Holman CSB)

I never understood where the idea came from that I could change someone else to fit me. That somehow I could change her from who she has become. I liked who she was enough to take an interest in her. What changed? Remember, she has had her lifetime thus far to become who she is today. What would make me believe that I could change her in a matter of days, months, or even years? Unfortunately, this is where many couples find themselves. One person makes it his or her goal to change something about the other. What we might see as a flaw, they might see as a strong characteristic. Would we want someone changing one of our strengths? No we would not.

A good example of this is compassion. Let us

assume that the husband has great compassion for helping others. However, compassion is not one of the wife's strengths; but being punctual is. The wife sees his compassion as making her late because he kept talking.

If someone wants to change, they will change on their own; the key word here is want. Outside sources can help, but the change must come from within. The wife of a friend of mine expressed to me this very thing. I asked her if this particular problem was a part of his personality when they met. She explained that he was like this in the beginning, but figured that he would change over time.

We cannot blame someone else because of our disbeliefs. If our mate was a certain way when we met, there is a good chance that part of his or her personality will not change. You have assumed and prejudged someone else based on what you want without fully taking them into consideration. The worst part, we now blame them for our unhappiness.

In the beginning, we knew this about our mate and we accepted it. We should not blame them for not changing as we had wished they would. My mother put it to me this way, "we all have our flaws. It is finding the flaws that you can live with." If this characteristic is not something we feel we can live with for the rest of our life, then we might want to reconsider settling down with this person. However, if we decide to accept it; then we must understand that we will be accepting it for the rest of our life. It is our own fault since we knew of its existence and accepted it from the start, and small things do not become huge things on their own. If it was only an irritant in the beginning, it should still be just an irritant. If two people are considering separation, after years of marriage because of it, then it was always more than just an irritant.

The good news is that by working together, the couple can work through anything that comes our way. First, give it over to God and allow Him to work from the inside out. It is a problem that neither of us could handle on our own. And, if a couple is considering divorce or separation, then that couple cannot handle it as a team either. I would recommend relying on His mighty power; open up to Him together. Through transparency with Him and each other, a solution will be presented. Second, take the stance that divorce is not an option. If this mentality is kept, assuming there is no physical or mental abuse occurring, we will be able to get through anything together (Matthew 19:26).

Chapter 16: "Why do I have to 'turn the other cheek' when I didn't do anything wrong?"

"If you love me, obey my commandments. And I will ask the Father, and He will give you another advocate, who will never leave you. He is the Holy Spirit, who leads into all truth. The world cannot receive Him, because it isn't looking for Him and doesn't recognize Him. But you know Him, because He lives with you now and later will be in you." (John 14:15-7; NLT)

Everyone, at some point in their life, is confronted with a situation where the best course of action would be to just walk away. Right before that decision is made, questions start flying. 'But, why do I have to walk away when I am not the one who started it?' 'Why do I have to be the bigger person?' In 2008, while stationed in Virginia, I was confronted with such a situation.

It occurred on a rather warm spring day. As most people know, the grass is going to grow and will need to be cut at least once a week. Getting ready to cut my grass, I checked my gas can and realized that I would need more. Since the gas station was nearby, I walked over to get a gallon. While I was standing there pumping my gas, an elderly man pulled his car into the slot that I was in. Again, I walked over so I did not have my car with me.

This man had seen me bent over pumping gas. However, with complete disregard for me and my well-being, he pulled up as close to me as he could and honked his horn. Naturally, I jumped when he did that. Not only because I was not expecting it, but because it was right in my ear. I guess I was in 'his' spot. I looked up at him and could see that he was yelling at me through his windshield. He was probably in his mid-fifties and of African American descent. I am not saying that race had anything to do with the situation. Rather, I am describing the individual.

I do not know where he was from, but where I come from pumping gasoline is first-come first-serve. After visibly yelling at me, he proceeded to pull his car next to where I was standing and continued to yell at me through the window. Instead of rolling down his window, he was yelling through it. I looked at him, and in as polite of voice as I could muster up stated, "I can't hear you." Then he said, "Don't worry, I'm getting out."

At this point, I stopped physically pumping gas just in case. I kept the nozzle in the gas can because I was not finished. The man got out of his car and proceeded to chastise me for being in his way. Then, he walked up to the pump and attempted to grab one of the other pumps. I could not figure out what I had done to deserve this verbal assault. One thing I did know, I was beginning to lose my temper with this man. When he approached me, my first thought went to self-defense. And, as everyone knows, the best defense is a good offense. But, I refrained from punching the old man. God definitely had His hand in the situation.

I explained to him that I was there first and I was using the pump. Even though I did not have my car, which was his primary complaint, I still had just as much right to that pump as anyone else. I further explained that it would not matter if I was on a motorcycle or a bicycle either. Some people just cannot be convinced that they are in the wrong.

After I finished pumping my gas, the man just would not relent. He continued to taunt me as if he wanted me to strike him. But, I turned my back and walked away. I know the golden rule says to treat others as you would like to be treated. In my anger, I had begun to treat this man as he was treating me. Once I realized that I had sunk to his level I stopped myself. At that point, I knew that I was just as much in the wrong as he was.

The next time we find ourselves in a compromising situation, remember that the Holy Spirit is with us always. When we do not know what to say, He will be our words. When we do not know how to act, He will guide our movements. And when we are ready to throw down, He will be our center of peace.

Chapter 17: "I will pray for you."

"For as the body without the spirit is dead, so faith without works is dead also." (James 2:26; NKJV)

Have you ever had someone say to you, or you have said to someone, "I will pray for you." Two things come to my mind right away. First, will that person who made the promise remember to actually pray for me? And second, will the person pray for my actual needs?

Even the most devout Christians forget things from time to time. There will be times where a person will take the time to write down your name and your problem. In my experience, those individuals are usually a part of a prayer team (not always though).

For those who do not know, a prayer team is comprised of church members who take time out of their days to pray for individuals, groups, activities, etc. Their prayers are not limited to just one or two people; they could be praying for the church body as a whole, political leaders of our country, and such. For instance, if they are in transition between senior pastors they might pray for a new leader. Perhaps the church is going through a physical change; expanding the worship, student center, or a whole new campus are some examples.

There are also fellow Christians who are not necessarily members of a prayer team but devoutly pray for others. In the Old Testament, it was mainly the leaders who would pray. Moses prayed for the Pharaoh and his people after each of the seven plagues of Egypt. When Jesus came, He taught everyone how to pray, using the Lord's Prayer as an example or template. The greatest prayer of all was the prayer Jesus Christ prayed to His Father for those who opposed Him (Luke 23:34).

Prayer is the strongest tool that we have as Christians. When someone tells us that they will pray for us, we should believe that they will. Whether they write down our problem/concern, or even our name, rest assured that we will be remembered. If even for a brief moment, we will come across their thoughts. It will be in that moment that a silent prayer will be lifted to God in our name.

Pray and ask others to pray as well. But do not stop there. We pray, others pray, and then we put action to those prayers; in that order. We are not to act and then pray that it works. First ask for God's help and then go to work. God cannot work through us if we are not willing to allow Him.

Chapter 18: "My friend is an active homosexual who believes in Christ. What does the Bible say about that?"

"For the law was not intended for people who do what is right. It is for people who are lawless and rebellious, who are ungodly and sinful, who consider nothing sacred and defile what is holy, who kill their father or mother or commit other murders. The law is for people who are sexually immoral, or who practice homosexuality, or are slave traders, liars, promise breakers, or who do anything else that contradicts the wholesome teaching." (1 Timothy 1:9-10; NLT)

This is like sex, religion, and politics, topics that too many people just do not want to talk about; as if the subjects are taboo. But, it is something that adult Christians need to talk about and understand. I believe it has a lot to do with America's stance on political correctness; specifically equal opportunity laws. This is not about the law of man; this is about the law of God.

In Paul's first letter to Timothy, he explained his role in spreading God's law to others. He was telling Timothy, as he tells us, that we should follow God's law as we follow the state's law. As long as we abide by them we have nothing to worry about. However, if we fail to follow the law there will be consequences. God's law started with the Ten Commandments that Moses brought down from Mount Sinai. Later Jesus expanded upon them.

Moses, prior to being called to do God's work, was a murderer himself, but God knew He could still use him. Moses was chosen to be the leader who would save the Israelites from slavery in Egypt. David, another party guilty of murder and adultery was also called to spread the word of God. Even though he was the youngest and smallest of his brothers, he would be a great King and one of the greatest leaders of the Bible. As with many others throughout history, these men were chosen to be great leaders of nations by God. He saw the best in them before they saw it in themselves. Even before they committed their crimes, God knew what they were capable of; because He created them.

Even though Moses did not make it into the promise land, we know that Moses was saved because he was with Elijah when Jesus took Peter, John, and

James to the top of the mountain (Matthew 17). Moses was chosen by God as a baby. God saved him from the slaughter and then watched over him his entire life. He knew His purpose for Moses and the people of Israel. He told Moses what to do, what to say, and Moses obeyed.

Moses and David each made mistakes when they committed their sins. However, they realized that they were wrong, repented from their sins, and made the decision to follow God. That is what God asks us to do when we sin, admit that we are sinners, ask Him for forgiveness, and then repent from our ways. If one continues to murder, steal, lie, practice sexual immorality, etc. then that person has not repented from their sins. If we ask for forgiveness but do not change our ways then we are going against God's law. If we go against God's law and decide to make our own law, as King Saul did, then we will fall out of favor with God.

We will be judged when we die for our actions while we were alive. If we believe in God and have accepted Jesus Christ as our personal Lord and Savior, but live a life of sin, we will be judged accordingly. Remember, we only fool ourselves if we know what God's word says but choose not to follow it (James 1:22).

Understand that if we continue in our wicked ways, we could lose favor with God. We all have sin within us. Because of the fall of man, we are born into sin. In order to be forgiven of this, God sent His son to be the sacrificial lamb on our behalf. When we believe in Him, our sins are covered by His blood. Through His blood, all sin can be forgiven. If we choose God, He gives us the strength to get through anything. To choose pleasures of the flesh over God is submitting to the devil's temptations.

We know that homosexuality is a sin, but one that can be forgiven. In 1 Peter 1:3-5, we read about God's mercy and hope for all believers. Our salvation cannot be taken from us nor will it ever fade. For those who believe, the sins committed have been covered by the blood of Jesus Christ and completely forgiven. Part of this caveat is that we must repent from our old ways and start over. Paul explains that if we do not, we will not inherit the Kingdom of God. Once we receive Jesus Christ as our savior, we become a part of His Kingdom. Therefore, we are not our own (1 Corinthians 6:9-10, 18-20).

If that does not mean anything to you, one could always think of what they did to homosexuals in the Old Testament. "If a man lies with a man as with a woman, both of them have committed an abomination; they shall surely be put to death; their blood is upon them." (Leviticus 20:13; NKJV)

Chapter 19: "I don't know if I can forgive a fellow believer. What should I do?"

"Then Peter came up and said to Him, 'Lord, how often will my brother sin against me, and I will forgive him? As many as seven times?' Jesus said to him, 'I do not say to you seven times, but seventy times seven." (Matthew 18:21-22; NKJV)

Wow, a powerful question that is hard to address. On one hand, the human instincts are to settle things in a physical manner. It would probably make us feel better by getting out the aggression through yelling or fighting. However, we also know that would not be the right course of action, but the hurt is so bad that we do not know if we can forgive that person either.

Jesus taught us a great deal of things during His short time on this earth. He taught us to love, cherish, forgive, show compassion, and to be slow to anger. What Jesus was saying is to continue to forgive our brothers and sisters. We sin every day against our Heavenly Father and every day He is willing to forgive us of our sins. Therefore, we are called to love one another and forgive each other. Not thinking of things of the earth but of things above (Colossians 3:2). Remember, as we must ask forgiveness from God so shall we ask for forgiveness from each other.

A lot easier said than done I agree. First, think about the greater aspect of life. With what that person did, was it so intense that our life will forever be altered? If not, then it is easy enough to forgive. If it is something so intense, like an affair with your spouse, then there may be many other issues to deal with as well.

Jesus forgave those who beat him, spat on him, and killed him. Death for us is a permanent event. But, the pain that we are going through right now is only temporary. If Jesus could forgive those who killed him, I think we could forgive someone for something that is only temporary.

Chapter 20: "I have tried talking to others about God and Christianity, but all I receive is grief in return."

"Go therefore and make disciples of all nations, baptizing them in the name of the Father and of the Son and of the Holy Spirit, teaching them to observe all that I have commanded you. And remember, I am with you always, to the end of the age." (Matthew 28:19-20; Holman CSB)

Not everyone is receptive to hear about God or Jesus Christ. We live in a free country, which means that we are free to believe whatever we want (referencing a higher power). Even though this country was founded on the principles of Christianity we, as a country, have gone away from that basic foundation. The way our forefathers founded this country was based on Christian principles. Even our Constitution and Bill of Rights were based on Christian beliefs. But, with freedom of religion (or freedom from religion) we have allowed our country to be changed by non-believers. Atheists believe that there are no gods. But, in believing there are no gods they are declaring they themselves are gods. That is their religion.

We are commanded to spread the Word of the

Lord (John 20:21). But, exactly how does one spread the Word? Many of us do not exactly know how to tell others about the wonderful things God has done. When I was taking an evangelism class at church, they discussed the idea of establishing a relationship/ common ground with the individual first. If the individual is a stranger, begin a conversation to establish a ground level trust. As the conversation continues we will find common interests with each other. This could take a few minutes or a few months to establish. The idea is not to rush it. We want to leave a lasting impression.

As Christians, we try to live our lives based on God's law and our faith in Him. Oftentimes, our actions and the way we live our life is more powerful than any words we could say. Before we begin trying to bring others to Christ, first make sure that we are not casting a false shadow. People can see through fake words through our actions. Some of the meanest and most disrespectful people I have ever met claimed to be

Christians.

Perhaps at one time they believed and practiced the Christian faith. However, at some point they turned away from Him. Just remember, we cannot lose him! He is always here with us, watching over us, caring for us, and loving us. Perhaps you have dealt with these types of people too (Job 35:3). We all live a life where sin is ever present. It surrounds us at all times. God never said living a righteous life would be easy. Because we believe in Jesus Christ we know two things. We are able to receive God's promise of eternal life. And we will never again have to face any of life's challenges alone.

Chapter 21: "What's the difference between Hollywood gossip and pornography?"

"For from within, out of a person's heart, come evil thoughts, sexual immorality, theft, murder, adultery, greed, wickedness, deceit, lustful desires, envy, slander, pride, and foolishness. All these vile things come from within; they are what defile you." (Mark 7:21-23; NLT)

Our society is fascinated with what goes on in Hollywood and the lives of celebrities. Who is dating who? Which actors are currently in rehab? And so on. Americans are so addicted that there are several magazines, websites, and television shows dedicated to this very topic. For a long time, whenever we would go to the grocery store, my wife had to stop and read the latest gossip.

A while back she realized that it was damaging and stopped buying them. I know I have caught myself looking at them. I do not pick them up, but I still read the cover at the store. When my wife used to buy them, I would look through them as well. I admit that I am guilty of falling into Satan's temptation.

Is there really a difference between this obsession with Hollywood and pornography, gambling, smoking, drinking or any other addiction? In my opinion they are all damaging in one way or another. And just like any other addiction, those who are addicted will first deny it or make excuses for it. 'I only read it for entertainment.' Or, 'I only read it when there's a long line at the store.' Even, 'I had to buy it because [whomever] had it too.'

The problem with this addiction is envy and lustful desires. We read these magazines and watch these shows to escape our own lives. 'I wish I had that' or 'I wish I looked like that'. When we start thinking in this manner we have become envious. We want what they have. Some are conceited enough to have convinced themselves that they should be on that cover. Saying things like, 'I'm more attractive than he/she is' or 'I can sing better than...' When we have these thoughts, we should humble ourselves and appreciate the gifts that we have been given. Either way, whether it is Hollywood gossip or pornography, they both can be damaging to families and society as a whole. In the end, one is not better or different than the other.

It is one thing to aspire to be an actor/actress, but it takes on a new meaning when we want to trade places with someone else. We are at the exact point in time and place on this earth where we are supposed to be. If we want to be an actor/actress then we should not give up that dream. Treat it as any other career. Go to school, network, and apply. If we just want to be wealthy, then we have made money our god.

Chapter 22: What Does It Mean To Speak In Tongue?

"And they were all filled with the Holy Ghost, and began to speak with other tongues, as the Spirit gave them utterance. Now when this was noised abroad, the multitude came together, and were confounded, because that every man heard them speak in his own language." (Acts 2:4, 6; KJV)

Saying the term 'speaking in tongue' might sound weird to some. If we were to ask the average person, what speaking in tongue means, they might conjure up a picture of a mystical experience. The experience is often captured on television during some national evangelist's yelling spree. The evangelist gives a compelling, and I might add a lot of yelling, sermon where people are jumping out of their chairs. Perhaps he walks over and lays his hand on a lady who was there for healing.

As the evangelist does this, the lady begins convulsing and speaking in a language that no one can understand; might sound more like mumbling than anything else. It would seem more like she was possessed by a demon and the evangelist was setting her free. Unfortunately, this is the image that has been portrayed far too often. Being filled with the Holy Spirit is a possession of sorts, but not one that would make the body go into convulsions.

When Jesus was baptized by John the Baptist in the Jordan River, the text tells us that the Holy Spirit came down and fell upon Him. Then the Heavens opened up and the Lord God spoke (Matthew 3:16-17). But, there is no mention of Jesus going into convulsions and blabbering. Even though it was still early in His ministry, Jesus commanded attention and had a great presence about Him. If He would have gone into convulsions it would definitely have been noted in scripture.

If we look in the book of Acts of the Apostles (Acts), after Jesus had been crucified and resurrected, the members of the early church were gathered together in an upper room when the Holy Spirit came upon them. In Acts 2:4, many interpret this as they began speaking in the unknown tongue (also known as the language of God and His Angels); a language that only

God, the Angels, and a chosen few can understand and interpret.

Well, there is some truth in that understanding. Since God made all of the people and languages of the world, He would in turn be able to understand them as well. Of course, His Angels would have that skill as well. The problem is that people read it out of context. If you continue in the text, in Acts 2:6, it explains that speaking in tongue refers to speaking in a known language.

The members of the early church were from all different places and backgrounds. They each had their primary (native) language, but they also spoke the same; they were bilingual. Scripture is telling us that they each spoke in their native language (tongue) and the others understood. It would be as if you were fluent in both English and Spanish, but English was your primary language. Insert yourself into the early church scenario, it would be similar to someone speaking to you in German (a language you do not know) but you heard it in English. That is what the text is saying.

If you look in 1 Corinthians, chapter 12, you will see the different gifts of the Spirit that each of us is given. Well, some are given what others are not so that we may use them together for His glory (1 Corinthians 12:7-11).

As you saw from Acts 2, the author referred to speaking in tongue as speaking in a known foreign language. If you ever find yourself speaking fluently in a language you otherwise do not know, then you are speaking in tongue. The same goes for someone who finds themself interpreting a language they had otherwise never known.

Chapter 23: "Is it okay to date/marry someone who is not a Christian?"

"Do not plant two kinds of seed in your vineyard; if you do, not only the crops you plant but also the fruit of the vineyard will be defiled. Do not plow with an ox and a donkey yoked together. Do not wear clothes of wool and linen woven together." (Deuteronomy 22:9-11; NIV)

A few of years before I married my wife Zoé, I dated a very nice young lady. We had a lot of fun dancing and talking together. But, I always felt like something was wrong. After I told my dad that we were dating, his first question was, "Is she a Christian?" At that time, I did not know what her beliefs were. To be honest, I never even asked her. I could not recall ever seeing her praying nor did I see any religious symbols. So, I asked her what her beliefs were. She told me that she was a Muslim.

My thoughts immediately jumped years into the future. I began to wonder how we would raise our children. I asked her if she would be willing to become a Christian. When she said no, I posed that question about the raising of any children that we might have.

She explained how I could take the kids to church with me. Why would you want to be married to someone only to do things separately?

Before I even thought of marrying Zoé, I had to know if she was a Christian or not. I married Zoé so we could do things together. We go to movies together; we go to dinner together; we hang out with our friends together; we go to church together; we pray together; and we sleep in the same bed. I realized that I could not be with someone who I could not do everything with.

When two believing Christians get married, they automatically start off with a stronger marriage. When a believer marries someone who is not a believer, then they are mixing two different seeds together. The fruits and crops, your children and marriage, will be defiled. That is not to say that Christians do not have a hard time; because they do. But, they also know that God is the glue between them. If you are not saved, look for someone who is a Christian that you might be saved through them.

We date people because we are looking for that one who will complete us. We all look for the one who will be our confidant, our friend, and our lover. Hopefully, this relationship will turn into something that will result in a long and loving marriage with beautiful children. Even if this person turns out to be perfect in every area, but is not a Christian, then we have gone against God's Word. That is why it is so important to make sure that we only date someone who is either a Christian or is willing to become one. This is not the time to find a 'project' to work on. Someone who is a professed atheist, agnostic, Muslim, or other religious beliefs, is not going to produce the fruits which we are seeking.

Now, if a mixed religion marriage has already been created, with or without children, it can still be rectified. First, the one who is not saved needs to ask to be saved and follow in believer's baptism. That person must be willing to accept God's gift. Then, we should dedicate to raise our Children in the way of the Lord. God is very loving and merciful, but He is also very jealous. He loves us very much and wants us to love Him in return.

Chapter 24: Which son are you?

"...All these years I've slaved for you and never once refused to do a single thing you told me to. And in all that time you never gave me even one young goat for a feast with my friends. Yet when this son of yours comes back after squandering your money on prostitutes, you celebrate by killing the fattened calf!' (Luke 15:29-30; NLT)

During Jesus' teachings, He loved teaching in parables. One very famous parable was of the prodigal son. Two thousand years later, we have made many movies and songs that reference the type of person described in the story. For those who do not know the story, Jesus taught about the youngest son of a wealthy man who demanded his inheritance. He took his money and left his home to go travel and party. He spent his money on drinking, partying, and sins of the flesh. Eventually, he ran out of money and his so-called friends; the ones who were with him during the partying, but left when the money ran out.

Penniless and homeless, the son of the wealthy man took a job feeding pigs. In those days, that was a very disgraceful job to have. Pigs were considered an unclean animal. One day, while feeding the pigs, he realized that even his father's servants lived better than he was. The young man swallowed his pride and headed for home. The young man thought, even if his father would not accept him, he would at least give him a job.

His father, the loving father that he was, did not say, 'I told you so.' He did not even put stipulations on his son's return. No, his father not only accepted him with open arms, but when he saw his son off in the distance he ran to him and embraced him. For the return of his lost son, the father had a huge celebration filled with food, music, and dancing.

Many stories capture that picture of a person who had everything, but at some point decided that they wanted to do everything on their own. The story helps us to see that the younger son had to lose everything in order to realize what he really had. But, what those stories do not talk about is the older son.

If you remember the parable, Jesus said that the

older son was envious of his younger brother. The older son became upset at his father for not throwing a party for him and his friends. While his brother was throwing away all of his money, the older son was working hard for their father. Every day, he was in the fields doing whatever his father asked of him. He was dedicated to doing his father's business.

The problem was the self-centeredness of the older son's heart. Since the younger brother had taken his inheritance and was out of the picture, whatever was left would be the older brother's. But, his heart became hardened when he returned from working in the field to find his father throwing a party for his younger brother. His sin occurred when he became angry and envious of his brother.

How many times have you worked hard and received no praise? How many times have you watched others do half the work yet they receive great rewards? Have you become jealous or envious of them for receiving success or rewards knowing that you had worked just as hard if not harder? Unfortunately, I know that I have been guilty of this. It is never easy to watch someone else being rewarded and we are not, especially when you both did the work. Or, when we watch them work harder to not work than it would have taken to complete the task.

But, God tells us to lay up our treasures in Heaven and not on earth (Matthew 6:19-20). Our reward will be given in Heaven for how we carry ourselves while on earth. Even though it would be easy to become upset or envious of the success of others, we need to be supportive and believe that our hard work has not gone unnoticed.

Let us ask, have we become jealous of our brother's reward? Or, have we realized that we have sinned against God and our father through our actions? Either way, we should humble ourselves and ask for forgiveness.

Chapter 25: You who are wealthy in the eyes of the world but poor in the eyes of God.

"Suppose a brother or sister is without clothes and daily food. If one of you says to him, 'Go, I wish you well; keep warm and well fed,' but does nothing about his physical needs, what good is it? In the same way, faith by itself, if it is not accompanied by action, is dead." (James 2:15-17; NIV)

Hopefully, by now you have a better grasp as to what your purpose is. But, now I think we should ask ourselves an even deeper question. Are we the kind of people who go to church every week, but we do not feel that we need to tithe (for whatever reason)? Or, perhaps we are the wealthy ones who put in an amount that is 'good enough' in our eyes even though it is not a tenth. We give excuses like we do not want to be the only one giving that much.

Let me help with something here, God owns it all. He does not need our money, because He already has it. No, what He wants is for us to love and trust Him. By giving Him a tithe, we are giving back to the One who gave it to us in the first place.

Perhaps we are the one who carries around a

couple hundred (or thousand) dollars in our wallet. Yet, when we see someone in need we walk by as if they were not there. We have more than enough to spare, yet we will not give even a dollar.

Abram did not need to give Melchizedek a tenth of everything he had recovered after defeating his enemies. Melchizedek was both the King of Salem and the High Priest. He was blessing Abram who had just returned from defeating King Kedorlaomer and his allies. In return, Abram gave the money as a form of worship.

Jumping forward a few thousand years to the time of Jesus Christ, His half-brother James spelled it out very clearly in the second chapter of James. I know that, as Christians, our most powerful tool is prayer. However, as James points out, faith without actions is dead.

At one point in my life, I had no job and did not know how I would pay for food or rent each month. The bad part, I was married with two small children. I had less than enough to put a roof over our head and food on our table. Each month was a struggle to get through. I prayed each day that God would provide the food for that day and the days to come. Every day, I prayed for enough money to keep a roof over our heads. And yet, I knew so many who were more than happy to tell me, 'I'll pray for you' and leave it at that.

These people believed that if they would only pray for me, then everything would be okay. But, someone must take action. Usually, that someone is the one who has the Holy Spirit telling them to help. It is that feeling inside urging you to do something. Unfortunately, many people never act upon it.

I did not ask for handouts. I wanted to work and provide for my family, but it was during a terrible time in the American economy. Of all the positions I applied for, I was either over qualified or under qualified. Even with all that, I did not give up on God or my responsibilities of being the head of the household. Every day, I prayed and believed that God would provide the food, the clothes, and the roof over our heads. And, I prayed and thanked God for the job He had in store for me; hoping that job would come soon.

If we tell someone who is down on their luck, 'I will pray for you' and we do nothing to help them, then what are we praying for? Are we praying that someone else would help them? How about we start praying for ways that we could help? God put us in each other's lives for a reason.

Chapter 26: I believe we have all doubted our faith at least once.

"Jesus said to him, 'I am the way, the truth, and the life. No one comes to the Father except through Me.'" (John 14:6; NKJV)

I was raised in a Christian household where we went to church every Wednesday and twice on Sunday. Every summer, I went to a youth church camp. That was just the way life was growing up.

At age thirteen, I accepted Jesus Christ as my Lord and Savior and followed in believers' baptism. I remember my dad drove the two hours so that he could baptize me in the camp pool. Even though it was more than twenty years ago, I can still remember it very clearly. It was a warm summer day, but I was still shaking from excitement and fear. All of the kids at the camp, well over one hundred, were all gathered around the pool to watch me get baptized. My dad asked me, 'Martin, do you believe that Jesus Christ is your personal Lord and Savior and that He died for your sins?' Without hesitation I replied, 'Yes.' And then he plugged my nose and said, "With that public profession of faith, I baptize you in the name of the Father, the Son, and the Holy Spirit," and lowered me under water and brought me back out again.

When I came up, all of the kids were clapping, yelling, whistling, and banging on the fence. There was a feeling that engulfed me that was extremely overwhelming to say the least. I still remember the goose bumps that raced over my entire body. I gave my dad a big hug and began to cry. It was an amazing day and event in my life. Unfortunately, in a few short years I would forget that feeling and begin to question why I believed at all.

Like a typical teenager, I began to question many things of life. But nothing like the way I questioned my faith. I felt like I only believed because I had been raised in a Christian household. I needed to figure out if I could believe without the influence of my family.

In high school, I began to seriously doubt my faith. It really took hold in one class where we were studying the major religions of the world. The one religion that was covered more than Christianity was Islam. So I asked myself the question, 'why do others believe in Islam?' I took a great interest to learn more about that religion. I think the thing that intrigued me the most was the similarities between Christianity and Islam. For instance, both religions started with Adam and include Abraham, Moses, and Jesus as main characters.

As an adult, I continued to learn about different religions in order to strengthen my own faith. For example, along with Islam and Christianity, Judaism also has Adam, Abraham, Moses and Jesus as key figures. Islam splits from Judaism when Ishmael and Hagar were cast out; Judaism and Christianity split at the resurrection of Jesus Christ. Ironically, both Islam and Judaism recognize Jesus Christ as a prophet; but that is where it ends.

To be a prophet one must live a life free of lies. If Jesus Christ was a prophet, and prophets cannot lie, then He must have been speaking the truth. Something else to think about, of all of the founders of religions (or religious leader), Jesus Christ was the only one who died and rose from the dead.

A modern newspaper or magazine requires at least two different accounts of an event to declare the information to be factual. Think on this, in the 40 days following His resurrection there were more than 500 eyewitness accounts of seeing Jesus Christ alive.

So I want you put yourself into the following scenario. You are walking down the proverbial road of life and you came upon a fork in the road. There is no clear choice as to which path you should take. At this fork there are two men there, one is alive and the other is dead. Which one will you ask for directions? Jesus Christ is alive and is the only one to overcome the grave as He had promised.

Chapter 27: What it means to be a man of integrity.

"Blessed is the one who perseveres under trial because, having stood the test, that person will receive the crown of life that the Lord has promised to those who love him." (James 1:12; NIV) "Let us not become weary in doing good, for at the proper time we will reap a harvest if we do not give up." (Galatians 6:9; NIV)

Unfortunately, there are many men and women in our society who lack integrity. First what is integrity? The easiest way to describe integrity is this way: integrity is doing what is right even when no one else is looking. Doing what is right when no one else is looking is important. However, I would like to take it a step further if I could. Doing what is right even if it means disciplinary action, punishment, or isolation.

When I was in Officer Candidate School (OCS) for the US Army, and when I worked for the railroad, at each location I was faced with an ethical dilemma. With OCS, it was the instructors physically abusing the students. In the railroad, it was my boss specifically instructing personnel, working on the facility, to violate railroad and federal safety rules.

Looking back on those situations, it would have

been a lot easier to just look the other way, like everyone else in my OCS class and on that railroad facility. But I am a man of integrity and I cannot just look the other way, especially when I know it is wrong. There are not many companies that will reward you for having integrity. Actually, it is more likely that the opposite will happen.

Paul and Jesus' half-brother James both have something to say about men of integrity. I have adopted those two verses as a way to live my life. Not only does a man of integrity do what is right, he speaks in the same manner; lies do not become us.

When I was a kid, I remember taking a $20 bill from my parents. I looked into the pouch of money full of $20 bills and thought, 'they won't miss this one'. About ten minutes later, my mother came to me and asked me, in the politest way possible, if I had taken the money. My flesh wanted to say, 'No!' And I knew that if I would have said yes that I would have received a good beating. Knowing that I could get a beating for taking the money, I went ahead and told my mother the truth. I grabbed the money and gave it back to her. I told her exactly what I had thought when I took it, "I didn't think you guys would miss it." But, they did miss it. Thankfully, I did not receive any punishment for taking the money. Instead, she expressed how she appreciated that I told her the truth.

God feels the same way about all of us. We are His children and when one of us goes astray He searches tirelessly until He finds us again. God loves you because you are His child. Regardless of your parents' love, He loves you even more. He has charged all men to be the head of their family as Jesus is the head of the church. As the head, we are called to always do what is right; especially during hard times.

As for me, I might not be a senior manager for the railroad because I would not look the other way. And, I might not be a company commander because I would not keep quiet. But, I know that God is watching down on me and He is proud of me. Remember,

He is always watching. What we do on earth builds our home in Heaven. If you are not saved, I would highly recommend that you become involved with a Bible believing church and get saved. Then, try to surround yourself with good Christian men (Proverbs 27:17).

We should not be afraid of thinking that we have done too much to be forgiven. God will forgive us regardless of what we have done; except for one; blasphemy of the Spirit of the Lord (Matthew 12:31-32).

Chapter 28: Are You On The Highway To Hell Or The Stairway To Heaven?

"Enter through the narrow gate. For wide is the gate and broad is the road that leads to destruction, and many enter through it. But small is the gate and narrow the road that leads to life, and only a few find it." (Matthew 7:13-14; NIV)

These are two great analogies of the truth. Highways are usually wide and vehicles are able to travel at high rates of speed to get to their destinations faster. Plus, many are made very wide to accommodate a high number of travelers. The lanes are wide so to accommodate cars, trucks, and even buses full of people. We want to get there fast!

However a stairway is usually very narrow, allowing only a small number of people to travel at any given time. Stairways also require much more individual effort than a highway. On a highway, individuals usually travel in vehicles where only the driver is doing the work. If you are the passenger, you can sit back and relax; maybe even get some shuteye. Even the driver has very little to do since the vehicle does most of the work. But, one must work hard to climb a staircase. Climbing stairs is exhausting, especially if there are numerous flights of stairs involved. Even on an escalator you have to stand the entire way.

That is life for most of us. We are either on a path of doing what is right, or we are on the path of wrong doings. It would behoove us to take a look at what we spend our money and our time on. One way to check this is to look at our checkbooks. Do we spend our time thinking of how we could make or spend more money? Maybe we are the type of people that always has to have the newest technical gadget on the market. Our closets are loaded with shoes and we cannot wait to get that next pair. Perhaps our jewelry box is spilling over. We could enjoy what we have, but we would rather get a larger jewelry box so we can fill it too. Or, do we think of how we can better the lives of those around us?

First, do we give our tithe to the body of Christ (the church) and His ministry? Please understand that God knows when we are going through hard times.

Perhaps we just lost a job, or some emergency situation just came up where we are unable to tithe. In that situation, we should think of giving of our time instead. Either way, it becomes an individual choice between us and God alone. No one else will judge us but God (Matthew 7:12).

When Jesus replied to the Pharisees, in Luke 20, He was giving us a great view of the difference between what is man's and what is God's. Asking for the coin, Jesus was signifying what came from man; what man had created (Luke 20:24-25). There is an old joke where God and a scientist are talking. The scientist tells God that he is just as powerful and can do anything that He could do. God says to the scientist, 'I made man from the dirt of the earth.' The scientist responds in kind, 'I can make man from dirt as well' and begins gathering dirt. God stops the scientist and says, 'no, go get your own dirt.'

Jesus further amplified His point in Matthew 7:21-23. That passage of scripture refers to the fact that not everyone who claims to know Him (be a believer) are actual believers. They say it but do not believe it. He clarifies this with the example of the two home-builders. One was a wise man who built his house on rock, while the other was foolish and built his house on sand.

He is telling us to listen to Him and put what He has taught us into practice; to be doers of the Word and not just hearers. We will inherit the Kingdom of God if we follow His teachings (Matthew 9:13).

Chapter 29: "I thought I knew what God wanted for my life. Was I wrong?"

"I cry out to Go Most High, to God who will fulfill His purpose for me." (Psalm 57:2; NLT)

That is definitely my story. I thought I knew that the Lord wanted me to provide for my family by taking a better job. The job led us to a new state and a new lifestyle. Unfortunately, ten months later I was no longer with the company. We had found ourselves in a state far away from family and without a source of income; not to mention in a house we could no longer afford. My wife and I decided to move back near family and start over.

One year later, we found ourselves in a similar situation again. My wife and I made a decision based on what I had felt God was calling me to do. Being the head of the household, it was my responsibility to provide for my family; to lead my family down life's journey toward prosperity. Throughout our journeys, God taught me some very important lessons.

In both instances, I was faced with both an

integrity dilemma and an ethical one. The first one, of course, was for the railroad. I was a middle manager at a railroad facility and was also in charge of safety for all personnel and operations. Unfortunately, my boss was much less concerned about safety and more concerned about the numbers and productivity. Needless to say we clashed heads. In the end, I stood my ground and lost my job.

The second instance was in Officer Candidate School (OCS); a leadership course in the Army. I was doing very well in my class; passing every test they threw at me and was succeeding with flying colors. Unfortunately, again I was faced with another dilemma. The instructors were taking advantage of their authority and physically abusing the students in the course. Because of the nature of the course, it was difficult for the students to say otherwise. However, I stood before the highest ranking officer in charge of the school and informed him of what was going on. For my actions, I was released from the program. Again, I was faced with the challenge and I stood my ground. If we do not stand for something, we will fall for anything.

Jesus and Job were both faced with difficult situations in which they were tested or tempted by the devil. In both cases, God knew what had to happen in their lives. He had seen the situations long before they came to light. God knew that they would stay true to who they were and who God is. But, there seems to be a common decision among society today to take an alternate route. The alternate route is to be a coward and turn the other cheek at the first sign of adversity.

Job lost everything for being a believer. During his trials, he did not turn on himself or on God. For his dedication, God gave him twice what he had before being tested. And Jesus, He was initially tested for forty days, and then for the following three years. In the end, Jesus gained what was already His; the world.

Being a Christian is not only about being a good person when others are looking. It is not only about going to church on Sunday. No, being a Christian is far more important than that. Being a Christian is about being ethical and moral, having integrity to do what is right, and being loyal even when it seems easier to go the other way.

I am sure many would say that one does not have to be a Christian to be a good person. But, just being a good person will not get them into Heaven (Ephesians 1:7-8). God gave us the wisdom and understanding to do what is right no matter the cost. Through Jesus' blood, He forgave us of our wrongdoings. Through His teachings, He taught us how to live and to make good choices; to do what is right even when it is hard.

Chapter 30: "What would you do to serve God?"

"Have I not commanded you? Be strong and courageous. Do not be afraid; do not be discouraged, for the LORD your God will be with you wherever you go." (Joshua 1:9; NIV)

Would you up and move your family to an unfamiliar place where you have no family, no friends, no place to live, and no job? I am not talking about what the gospels of Jesus Christ and His disciples did two-thousand years ago. I am not even talking about missionaries who go into foreign lands to spread the gospel. At least they have financial support from independent donors and churches. No, I am talking about something else. In 2010, God called me to up and move my family to the very place I described.

In 2009, I began preparing for my 2010 separation from the Army. I knew it was going to be a tough transition. In 1998, I was unprepared when I left active duty Army the first time. Remembering what I had gone through before, I wanted to be prepared this time. I began talking to people and creating a network. The more people I talked to, the more one thing became a common factor; 'Go to San Antonio.' Or, 'San Antonio is where the jobs are.'

At first, I did not think anything of it. With the advancement of technology and the internet, I was able to search all over the country, even the world, looking for my next career after the military. Throughout my search, San Antonio continued to come up. When I first told my wife that I was thinking of moving us to San Antonio, she thought I was crazy. "We don't know anyone in San Antonio," she said. She further amplified that by saying, "If you want to go, that's fine. You can send me a postcard." I was a bit discouraged, so I kept looking elsewhere.

Sometime in late 2009, my wife became ill with the flu. A friend of ours from church gave her an mp3 player filled with 'healing scriptures'. Listening to her new device, she began to find comfort in the scriptures. The more she listened, the better she felt. One day, I looked at the device to see who was providing the divine wisdom. The device had the name of a church located in San Antonio, TX on it.

As I networked with different people, the suggestions for San Antonio continued to flow in. At about that time, Zoé was going through a Bible study on the women of faith. They were studying in the book of Esther when she received confirmation to trust God. She realized that He was trying to work through me. Once she made the decision to follow me in the venture, we began to tell people that we were relocating to San Antonio. Several people kept telling us that either they had been there and loved it, or that they knew someone who lived there. This does not include the many who themselves were from there and planned to return. It was overwhelming. When God speaks in repetition like that, it is imperative to follow His guidance.

Unfortunately, the fact remained that I still did not have a job. We still did not have a place to live. And, we still did not know anyone. Before leaving Virginia, I reserved a hotel room for one month. We took whatever we could fit in our vehicles with us, the rest we put into storage. I believed that since God had led us to San Antonio, I would have a job and we would be moving into the house of our dreams in just two weeks.

It was an eye-opening realization that we work on God's timing, not ours. After living out of suitcases in a small hotel room for a month, money was running low. I still did not have a job or any possible opportunities. I knew full well that we could not buy a house without a job. So, my wife and I talked it over and decided the best thing for our family would be to move back home. We might be defeated, but we would be able to stay with family until we got back on our feet. That decision took place on a Friday afternoon.

We decided that we would go to church Saturday night and then travel all day Sunday. That way we could be back home by Monday. I woke up extra early Sunday morning and loaded both vehicles to head back home. Before leaving, we realized that Samuel (who was sixteen months old at the time) would need some more milk. Additionally, we would need ice for the cooler and I needed gas for my vehicle.

That morning, with all of the stress of the move we had an argument. Neither of us were happy that we had to tuck our tails and retreat back to the security of family. Our pride probably got the best of us that morning. One of the excuses she used for the argument was the way I had loaded her vehicle. My thoughts were, 'well, if you didn't like the way I loaded it, then you should've gotten up and loaded it yourself.'

As the time came for us to head out, I suggested that she go to the store ahead of me. While there, she could reload her vehicle the way that would make her more comfortable. It would also give me the chance to get gas. We kissed, said we were sorry, and she headed to the store. As I was began to drive out of the hotel parking lot, my vehicle sputtered and died. That was not a good sign, especially since we had nearly 900 miles ahead of us.

Since the oil light had come on, I checked the oil level; it was low. I try to keep a spare quart of oil in my car just in case. I put the quart in and started it up again. This time it seemed fine. I headed out to get gas. Nearly half way to the gas station my vehicle began to overheat. It was a hot day out, so I had the air conditioner blowing. Immediately, I turned off the A/C and rolled down the windows. That helped out a bit, but it was still not enough.

After I pulled into the gas station, I checked my coolant level to find that my overflow was completely empty. However, I had to wait until I got to the store to get some antifreeze. Thankfully, the store was not that far from the gas station.

There was a lot of traffic that day. As long as I kept moving, the airflow would keep the engine cool. But, when I had to stop the vehicle would start overheating again. Thanks be to God, I eventually made it to the store. I saw Zoé and waved to her as I walked into the store to get the supplies.

Since my wife had made it there before me, she was already reorganizing her vehicle. She was also making trips to and from the trash can. It was during one of those trips that a lady stopped her to ask if she needed any help. The lady had seen how my wife's vehicle was loaded to the top with stuff; next to her was Isabela (who was five at the time) trying to help her re-organize it. By that point my wife was distraught. Here we were about to leave the place we felt God had led us to. We had been living in a small hotel room for a month, and to add insult to injury, I had not received even a hint of a job offer.

The kind lady, Stephanie, proceeded to tell my wife her story of when she got to San Antonio. "I've been there before," she said. "Right where you are now." She went on to say that when she moved to San Antonio with her family, they had no place to live, no money, no job, and no friends or family to help.

By that time, I had purchased the items and made my way out to my vehicle. I parked near her vehicle so we could leave together. I put the antifreeze in my car and started it up to let the coolant run through the system. In the meantime, I took the milk and ice over to Zoé's vehicle. After about five minutes, I went back to check on my car; it was still overheating.

I turned off my vehicle and went over to find out who Zoé was talking to. She introduced me to Stephanie. We shook hands and she began to tell me her story. She suggested that we go to the apartment complex where she was living; the same place she went when she had nowhere else to go. She explained how they really helped her out when she had nothing. I said, "But, I don't have a job." She responded, "It doesn't matter, they will work with you." I said, "But we don't have great credit." She said, "Neither did we. But, these people are there to help you have a place to call home."

We told her that we had visited that apartment complex before and had really liked them. However, they did not have any three bedroom apartments available. Since we have two children, one boy and one girl, we wanted a three bedroom place to live. Stephanie suggested that we consider moving into a two bedroom apartment until a three bedroom became available.

My wife and I were so focused on a three bedroom, that the thought of anything less had never entered our minds. We decided that we would pray about it and thank God for sending Stephanie to us. Since we were already two and one-half hours late leaving, we decided to go to the apartment complex and see what they had to offer. Mind you, this was the only apartment complex open on Sundays.

After making the decision to go, and praying, we went back to our vehicles. The matter of time for our talk and prayer was less than ten minutes. When I started up my car, the temperature was back to normal. I knew immediately that God was making it clear that He was not through with us in San Antonio.

We went to the place, filled out the application, and were able to move in the very next day. Because all of our things were still in storage, we had to sleep on the floor. The following day, we purchased an inflatable mattress and folding chairs. We knew that God's Will was more important than our comfort. Eventually, we had all of our stuff shipped from storage.

I have talked to many people who could not believe that we made the move. We had decided to follow God's Will for our lives. So I ask you, what are you willing to do to serve God?

Chapter 31: So, what is my purpose in life?

"According to the grace given to us, we have different gifts; If prophecy, use it according to the standard of faith; if service, in service; if teaching, in teaching; if exhorting, in exhortation; giving, with generosity; leading, with diligence; showing mercy, with cheerfulness." (Romans 12:6-8; Holman CSB)

In order to figure out what our purpose in life is, we must first figure out what God's purpose is. God created the Heavens and the earth. God created night and day. And God created everything that was, is, and is to come. God loves each and every one of us for He made us in His image. And all He asks is that we love Him in return. He sent His one and only Son to teach us how to live, how to give, and then He died a painful death that our sins might be forgiven. Jesus taught us that we are to teach the gospel everywhere and to everyone (Ephesians 4:12). That is God's purpose for you (Acts 17:26-27).

In order to find your purpose in that equation, I would recommend that you figure out what your personal strengths are. There are many spiritual gifts tests available, but for the abbreviated version, identify what it is that you love to do. If you are the type of person that loves to talk to others, perhaps you could talk to everyone you meet about the great things God has done for you; better referred to as evangelism. Perhaps you could be a Sunday school teacher or hold Bible studies in your home.

If you do not enjoy talking to others, there are many things for those who are more of an introvert. Perhaps God has given you the gift of creativity. You could be creative for Christ; through art, marketing, advertising, or the like. Maybe you love to quilt; you could quilt for Christ. There are so many possibilities, but that is something you will need to figure out on your own.

It does not matter if you are an extrovert or an introvert. Nor does it matter what occupation you have chosen in life; or what occupation life has chosen for you. Everyone has at least one spiritual gift that God has provided. Use your gifts or gifts to glorify God whatever they may be. In doing so, you will be fulfilling your purpose in life. Remember, you can either be one of a million or one in a million.

Food for thought, as Christians, we have been instructed to spread the Word (Mark 16:15). One word of advice, find out what your greatest strength is and focus on that. Do not try to do numerous activities in an attempt to determine your purpose. Find one thing and concentrate your energy into that. You probably already know your greatest gift. Use that to your advantage and find ways to use your talents for His glory, for His Kingdom and for His people.

Appendix A:

<u>I Will Pray For You</u>
By Martin G. Howard

This morning, I woke up early to start the day;
I sat in silence and prayed that You would have Your way.
Every day is a trial just to get through;
Thankfully I have someone to trust in, someone like You.
A man whom I did not know, saw my pain;
We began to talk and he asked for my name.
After our talk, he said this is what I will do;
He closed his eyes and said I will pray for you.
Jesus, have Your way with this man;
Alone he is unable, but with You he can.
Come into his heart and have Your way;
That through You he will have a better day.
God love him as he is weak;
For this man is one of your lost sheep.
I will pray for you when you are weak;
And I will pray for you when you are strong.
I will ask God for your forgiveness;
For it is in His Kingdom that we all belong.

Appendix B:

Clothe your brother and feed your sister

By Martin G. Howard

A man, down on his luck.

He had the love but lost it somehow.

Now, he sits alone wondering where he went wrong.

What he did to lose it all.

Another man, full of life and living rich

passes him by on the street.

The rich man stops and asks him his name.

Ashamed, he can't look in the rich man's eye.

The rich man says, I will pray for you and walks on by.

Thank you for your prayers, he said,

but could you spare some bread?

You wish me well and turn away.

Jesus said, clothe your brother and plant the seeds

Love your sister and feed her needs

What good have you done, if you just wish them well?

The rich man stopped and said to him,

take my coat

take my money

you can have many things

But, without my God you will never have His wings
Jesus said, clothe your brother and plant the seeds
Love your sister and feed her needs
What good have you done, if you just wish them well?

"Battle of the Spirits"
My Personal Testimony

"A man who endures trials is blessed, because when he passes the test he will receive the crown of life that God has promised to those who love Him.." James 1:12; Holman CSB

I had never thought of myself as an alcoholic. When I used to drink, I never drank to get drunk. I merely drank to feel that buzz; perhaps even to numb the pain of everyday life. In 2009, while serving on active duty Army, I would get home from work and almost immediately pour myself a drink. It was just a habit. I began drinking right away because I did not want to get called back into work. I knew if I had been drinking they could not call me in until the necessary time had passed. My work had become so bad that I had to drink in order to avoid it.

I had been drinking most of my adult life. My drinking consisted of one maybe two drinks a night on the weekends. When I was in my mid-20's I probably had a little too much once in a blue moon. On those nights, I found myself praying to the porcelain god (the toilet bowl). I never made a habit of getting drunk because I hated the way it felt.

Backing up a little bit. When I was 19, I married the girl I had been dating during high school. I also joined the Army that year. My first duty station was in the beautiful rain forest country of Panama. It was a beautiful country and I loved my job. Because we were living in a foreign country, my ex-wife was bored all day; in turn, she made my life miserable.

After nearly a year in Panama, we were relocated to Texas. During our time there, I was deployed several times. While I was gone, my ex-wife would be unfaithful with numerous men. Of course, I did not find out about it until a few years later; at the end of our marriage. Since I was raised in a Christian household, marriage was very important. Even though she had been unfaithful, I insisted that we work things out.

We returned back home to Nebraska after I left active duty in 1998. In 1999, after nearly six years of marriage, my ex-wife and I separated; the divorce was finalized in 2000. Even with all of those problems, I still did not drink much. I did not need alcohol to take care of my problems. Alcohol was just a way to pass the time. In 2002, I finished my bachelor degree and then in 2003 I remarried; this time to the love of my life. My life was getting much better.

In 2005, my wife and I brought into the world our first child. It was a glorious time. Our daughter was so beautiful and I knew that it was my responsibility to be the best daddy a man could be. So our daughter would know how a man should treat a woman, I also knew that I had to be the best husband. During that time, I was drinking one to two drinks once or twice a week; usually over dinner.

In the beginning of 2006, the railroad, that I had been working for since January 2004, promoted me and sent us to Utah. Immediately, my hours went from 55 hours a week to 85 hours a week. I was spending more time at work than anything else, including sleeping.

About two months after we got there, I was

faced with an ethical dilemma at work. Do I turn my back on many major safety violations, like the railroad wanted me to do? Or, do I stand up for what was right? Being the ethical and moral man that I am, I stood up for what was right.

After six months of trying to make safety a priority over productivity, the railroad did not see that as the right decision; I was let go. For the first time in my life, I did not just go with the flow. I stood tall and proud for what was right. I had my legs chopped out from under me for doing what was right. But, I kept my head held high. By the end of 2006, we had sold our home, half of our belongings, and moved back to Nebraska.

Once back in Nebraska, I tried my hand in insurance sales. It did not take long for me to realize that I was not going to be a good insurance salesman. I would look at prospective customer's policies and realize that they were better off with their current provider. Well, I knew that I would never make any money looking out for prospective client's best interest. So, I left the insurance industry.

In June 2007, my wife and I made the decision to rejoin the military. I explained to her, when I go back into the military, our family will also be going into the military. Deployments, relocations, and the daily life in the military involve the entire family not just the service member.

Being former enlisted, I knew that if I was going back into the Army I would only go in as an officer. Enlisted and officers are treated completely different. It could be compared to having the choice between a hamburger and a New York Strip steak. There is no comparison.

Because I already served in the Army, and had a bachelor degree, I decided to get my commission through the Officer Candidate School (OCS). The program was only three months long, and upon completion I would have my commission.

Within the first three weeks, I could already see

the writing on the wall. I knew that I would be faced with yet another ethical dilemma. The instructors, or cadre as they are called, were physically abusing the candidates; I mean they were punching, kicking, choking, and pushing us. That does not include the allegations of cadre having sexual relations with the candidates either. It was bad. As you might have figured out by now, I would not stand for it.

In my stance to right the wrong, at week eight of the fourteen week program, I went in front of my company commander (CO), and later the battalion commander (BC). I informed them of the situation. For my actions I was dropped from OCS. The charge was, "Unbecoming of an officer candidate". I guess I was supposed to just sit back and keep quiet like the rest of my class (Class 505-07).

After I was dropped from the program, I spent the next two months waiting to receive my permanent change of station (PCS) orders. During that time, the BC had an internal investigation performed based on my complaints. Because it was internal, it resulted in nothing.

I received PCS orders to Virginia; I would serve out the remainder of my three year contract there. It was pretty obvious that I was frustrated and beaten down. I lost a job at a major railroad because I did what was right. Then, I lost my commission in the United States Army for doing what was right. In both situations, it would have been much easier for me to turn my back. I could have let the safety violations continue, which I am sure they did. And, I could have let the cadre continue to beat the candidates, which I know they continued to do. But, I knew that I could not in all consciousness just stand by and let that happen.

By late 2007, I had a major chip on my shoulder. I signed up to be a commissioned officer, but I found myself back as an enlisted soldier. I did not come back in to the Army to be an enlisted soldier. I never forgot how poorly they are treated. No, I came back in to be an officer because I also knew how they are treated.

Over the next year, even though I hated going to work I made the best of it. I was very happy at home with my wife and daughter. We had found a great church and were making some wonderful friends. In early 2008, my wife and I realized that we were expecting our second child; this time it was a boy. We were filled with joy in anticipation of increasing our family. But, we were also concerned since my wife had so many complications with the first pregnancy. Our daughter had been born three months early. And, my wife had spent one month in the hospital prior to her birth. We decided that she would finish her pregnancy with a specialist back in Nebraska, since the military only allows you to use military doctors; which are neither good nor consistent.

And then a third disappointment was on the horizon. In November 2008, the Army Human Resources Command (HRC) had put me on PCS orders to go to the state of Washington. The orders were to join a unit and deploy to Afghanistan with them. Because of the uncertainty on how the pregnancy would go, I could not up and move across country. That meant that I could not accept the orders.

Knowing this, I contacted HRC and explained the situation. The unfortunate truth is that they really do not care about why a soldier is unable to accept a set of PCS orders; they need to meet their numbers. Eventually, I contacted my senator requesting help; he gave a half try with no success. When I say half try, I mean like trying to pick up a weight, but stopping as soon as you grab it. My senator contacted HRC; when they gave him a half-truth he accepted it as set in stone and sent me up the river.

In January 2009, HRC gave me an ultimatum, re-enlist and accept the orders to move to Washington and deploy. Mind you, my family would not be a part of the move since they were in Nebraska. They would not be able to say goodbye to friends. They would not be able to grab anything that they might need for the next two years (since that was how long I would have been gone).

My other option was to sign a declination statement (better known as a 'dec statement') declining to re-enlist. If I signed the dec statement, I would be sealing the end of my Army career. I would no longer be able to attend any military courses. I would no longer be able to get promoted. Additionally, I would lose all transition benefits. These are benefits the military awards personnel as they transition out of the service back to society. And, if I wanted to re-enlist at a later date I would not be able to.

I went back into the Army to take care of my family, not to be away from them all of the time. By that time, we had already been apart for more than thirteen months cumulatively. I was not going to move to Washington without my family, and then be deployed from them for another 12-18 months.

In a few weeks, I flew back to Nebraska to welcome our son into the world. Unfortunately, the worries I had about my wife's pregnancy had come true. She had pre-Eclampsia before our son was born. After the traditional four days of recovery, she was sent home. She was home for one day when she had to go back in.

Once our son was born, her body took a turn for the worse and she had to spend another week in the hospital. After that week, she had convinced the doctors to let her go home to be on bed rest. She wanted to spend time with me before I had to head back. One week after she was discharged from the hospital I returned to Virginia.

Once again, I found myself alone in the house. Work had become even worse than before. I started getting treated differently because I signed the dec statement. I was not respected as I had been before. Nothing about me as a person had changed, but everything had changed because I signed that document.

With everything that was going on, I began drinking heavily. Instead of one to two drinks a couple nights a week, I started drinking two to three drinks every night. In order to drink, I would make excuses not to go out; that included going to church. On a few occasions, I even missed choir practice because I felt I needed to drink instead. It continually got worse. My two to three drinks became three strong drinks, and with each drink I started adding more and more alcohol. In actuality, I was probably drinking six to seven drinks a night.

It did not really get bad until October 2009 when depression set in. I had reached a point where I hated going to work. That was a big transition from once enjoying going to work. I used to feel like I was making a difference. But that time was gone. Now, because of who I had to work for, I hated the idea of going to work. Since I was not in his clique, my boss was extremely hard on me. I would do just as much work, if not more, than others. Yet, I would not receive the same rewards.

My wife could see that I was drinking a lot; she

knew that I needed help. She began to make subtle hints that I might be drinking too much. She even suggested that I talk to somebody about my drinking. Her complaining made me not want to be at home either. I did not want to hear what she had to say; after all, the alcohol was my coping mechanism. I was losing who I was as a person, as a husband, as a father, as the head of the household, and as a Christian.

My wife suggested that I see a counselor because she felt that I was depressed. She told me that the church would even pay for it if we could not. After many times of hearing that from her, I finally decided that I would see a doctor. The doctor agreed with my wife; I was depressed. He prescribed Prozac for me and sent me out the door. The doctor did not want to set up counseling appointments. He did not suggest any ways that we could make me better other than medication. Nope it was, 'here is a prescription for an antidepressant, now go away'.

The Prozac curbed my irritability, but it did not

slow my drinking. If anything it helped increase it. The drug states specifically on the bottle not to take with alcohol, but that is exactly how I would take it. I would make myself a drink and down the pill.

As I got closer to the end of my enlistment contract, I began making more doctors' appointments. I wanted to get all of the injuries I sustained in the Army documented. That is a normal part of the transition process. Unfortunately, it brought even more heat from my superiors because I was gone to my appointments. It was a never-ending cycle with them. Even though, while I was at work I would work harder than most. I accomplished more than most, but it was still not good enough. They would rather have me there doing nothing than be at my appointments.

Eventually, I went back to the doctor and explained that the Prozac was no longer working for my irritability and anger. He switched me over to a different antidepressant called Wellbutrin. Within a week, my desire to drink had subsided. Actually, when I would try to have a drink it would leave a really bad taste in my mouth. I would actually pour out half or more of the drink.

Another part of the transition process is the opportunity to submit a disability claim through the Veterans Affairs department. I was submitting for all of my injuries and my depression. To confirm my claims, I had to attend five different appointments; a full physical and four specialty clinics. One of the specialty clinics was for depression. During my visit with the psychiatrist, she told me that I suffered from anxiety, built up anger, and that I was an alcoholic. Prior to that day, I did not feel that I was an alcoholic. I mean, I just drank alcohol to help me relax. It was not like I was addicted to it or anything; or so I thought.

After my meeting with that psychiatrist, I began to take notice of my life. I remember going home one day after work and reaching for a bottle of rum. It was almost out of instinct that I did it. There was no real thought put into it. It was at that point that I realized that the doctor was right. I had become dependent upon the alcohol. I literally stood there with my arm extended fighting an internal battle. I wanted a drink so bad, but I also knew I had to resist the temptation.

I had been filling myself with plenty of spirits, but I was not filling myself with the Holy Spirit. Jesus said, "Everyone who drinks this water will be thirsty again, but whoever drinks the water I give him will never thirst. Indeed, the water I give him will become in him a spring of water welling up to eternal life." (John 4:13-14; NIV)

I have gained a control over my desire for alcohol; it no longer controls me. I have a refreshed view on life. My eyes are no longer hazed from alcohol or anger. I no longer need alcohol to soak away my sorrows. I had resorted to alcohol to escape everything. Now, I have embraced doing what is right even when it is the unpopular thing to do. I understand that I will be rewarded by God for my actions. "Let us not become weary in doing good, for at the proper time we will reap a harvest if we do not give up." (Galatians 6:9; NIV)

I truly hope I have helped you to find your purpose.

Feel free to email me at **mypurpose2012@yahoo.com**. I would love to hear how this book has helped you and/or a loved one.

Check out the website at: www.mypurpose2012.webs.com.

Also check on my book, "Where the Alley Turns Cold", available at most online retailers.